Stamp Collecting as a Hobby

Burton Hobson

FOREWORD BY WILLIAM C. MENNINGER, M.D.
EDITED BY ROBERT OBOJSKI

Sterling Publishing Co., Inc.   New York

COIN & STAMP BOOKS

Coin Collecting as a Hobby	How to Build a Coin Collection
Coin Collector's Price Guide	Stamp Collecting as a Hobby
Historic Gold Coins of the World	Stamp Collector's Price Guide

Catalogue of the World's Most Popular Coins

ACKNOWLEDGMENTS

The author wishes to thank Dr. William C. Menninger for his foreword evaluating stamp collecting as a hobby and Stamps Magazine for permission to reprint the article.

Special thanks are due H. E. Harris & Co., Minkus Publications, Inc., Scott Publications, Inc., and the Grossman Stamp Co., Inc. for their cordial cooperation in supplying pictures of their products. The section on topical collecting owes a great deal to the helpful suggestions of Glen Larson and thanks are due Moe Luff for his help.

Many of the stamps pictured were supplied by George Marshall of the West Toledo Coin Shop, and by Robert Obojski from his personal collection.

Library of Congress Cataloging-in-Publication Data

Hobson, Burton.
   Stamp collecting as a hobby.

   New ed. of: Getting started in stamp collecting.
   Rev. & enl. 1982.
   Includes index.
   1. Postage-stamps — Collectors and collecting.
I. Obojski, Robert. II. Hobson, Burton. Getting started in stamp
collecting. III. Title.
HE6215.H6   1986   769.56'075   86-6015
ISBN 0-8069-4794-2
ISBN 0-8069-4795-0 (lib. bdg.)

CONTENTS

Foreword

by William C. Menninger, M.D.

Stamps have many advantages over almost anything else, as collectible items. They are commonplace articles of everyday life, making them easily accessible and available to everyone, everywhere. Being paradoxically both cheap and valuable, thousands are available for a cent apiece while others cost many dollars. The fact that their value gradually appreciates (in a few romantic instances to fabulous figures) adds to their appeal to collectors and constant world demand assures their resale.

The compactness of stamps is an important advantage over most other collectible items. Their esthetic value appeals to some, their historical interest to many, and their geographical relationships to almost every collector. Probably the greatest attractions for the serious collector are the many bypaths which lead from stamps: the study of history, transportation, industry, manufacturing, science.

These reasons for stamp collecting's popularity concern themselves with the media itself and not with the more fundamental, psychological satisfactions. Of these, the most obvious perhaps, is the opportunity stamp collecting gives for amassing a large number of specially treasured objects in which one can invest energy, time, and money—and which become part of himself.

It is the exceptional stamp collector who ever becomes satisfied with the number of stamps he has accumulated. Furthermore, most stamp collectors are not seriously interested in parting with their stamps. They may do so in exchange, but this is only to accumulate new acquisitions for their collection. The desire to accumulate, enlarge, and hold on to stamps is a characteristic fundamental to most collectors.

Another psychological value is the opportunity in stamp collecting for precise arrangement of acquisitions, with special attention to orderliness and completeness. Every stamp collector is apt to have a mass of unsorted and disarranged stamps to begin with, and his chief satisfaction is gained from arranging his collection in some kind of systematic order: chronologically, by subject, type, similarity, or color. He is continuously looking for specimens he needs to complete a certain arrangement. When he "needs" a particular stamp or stamps, he seeks these in contacts with his collector friends and his dealers. He compulsively makes lists and marks his catalogue to remind himself of his needs.

Thus stamp collecting furnishes an ideal outlet for compulsive activity and there is unlimited opportunity to express an interest in detail. Variations in shades of color, different types of the same stamp, errors and flaws in printing, variations in watermarks and perforations are all examples of this opportunity to study detail. Closely related is the opportunity to study the stamps themselves, as suggested by their particular usage, country of origin, or subject matter. Every collector must carry out his own investigation in identifying each stamp, and many advanced collectors find research activities in connection with their particular specialty.

Stamp collecting serves as both a solitary and gregarious activity. During the war years, stamp collecting activity increased because wartime conditions kept many people at home. On the other hand, there are hundreds of philatelic groups in existence which bring collectors *together* for exhibits, programs, auctions, buying and selling, trading and—probably most of all, just for fun.

Introduction

The postage stamp is one of the world's great achievements. Before stamps, the sender of a letter did not pay postage, and the recipient had to pay cash-on-delivery for the service before he knew what the letter contained. This was an unsatisfactory procedure, one that led to many complaints. Can you imagine what the life of a postman would be like today, if he had to stop and collect for every letter and package he delivered?

(Left) The Penny Black, the world's first adhesive postage stamp, on its 100th anniversary was reproduced on a stamp of Mexico. Used copies of the actual 1840 stamp sell for about $200 today.

Another early stamp, the "Post Office" Mauritius issue, also shown on its centennial. Originals of this issue are worth at least $250,000! The stamp shown costs about 25¢.

The first postage stamp was used in 1840, when Rowland Hill of Great Britain (later awarded a knighthood for his achievement) succeeded in establishing a uniform penny rate for letters sent anywhere within the United Kingdom. The penny postage scheme applied only to letters that were paid for in advance and the adhesive postage stamp was introduced as a sort of receipt to show clerks and carriers that the postal fee had been collected.

The idea was so successful that the United States adopted it in 1847, and by 1860 the use of adhesive postage stamps had spread to most of the civilized nations of the world. Today, stamps and mail are available to people everywhere and you only need to read and write to participate in the great world of communication by mail. Few places on earth are too remote to be reached by mail.

Today the postman is taken for granted as a part of our daily life, and postage stamps are so widely used that most people seldom give them a glance. Yet, if you look at a stamp closely, you will discover the whole world is in it—right at your door. For that bit of adhesive paper may come from the far corners of the earth, may show a picture of a nation's hero you never knew about, or the product of a land you only knew from stories. It may portray life in that country, food, dress, a festival, a sports event, a ship, a mountain. And it will undoubtedly tell you (if it is a foreign stamp) of a currency that differs from your own.

1. Stamps Bring the World to Your Door

Stamps recall history

With the help of stamps you can wander through lands, time and history. On a stamp expedition you can discover how things looked years ago. The traditional ways of life are dying out in our modern world, but they are preserved for us on stamps. The important events of the past, including the history of our own country, are recalled by special commemorative issues.

Famous people from all walks of life appear on stamps. (Left) Actress Grace Kelly and Prince Rainier. (Center) Author Robert Louis Stevenson. (Right) Inventor Thomas A. Edison.

A stamp collection presents a picture gallery of great people of all times—rulers, statesmen, warriors, explorers, artists and scientists —as well as their achievements and adventures. Stamps invite further study—you will want to know about the people, places and things that are shown, why they were selected, what their significance is.

Stamps are works of art

Stamps have been in use for just over 135 years but the number printed in that time runs into the billions. The first stamps were very plain. They showed the portrait of a sovereign or president, the coat of arms of a nation, while some had merely a mark of value.

Early stamps were usually very plain. Most recent issues are colorful pictorials; some are "modern design" compositions.

Most modern issues, however, are beautiful, multi-colored pictorials. Because great care and expense goes into their design and production, they are often miniature works of art. The designs range from modernistic compositions of form and color to stamps with intricate arrangements of borders, frames and scrollwork. All the colors of the rainbow have been used, sometimes many colors on a single stamp. One pleasure of stamp collections is to look through an album stamp by stamp and enjoy the particular beauty of each one.

These Formosa butterflies are shown in full color on the actual stamps. These multi-color pictorials add to the appeal of collecting and the appearance of your album pages.

The fact that governments issue the stamps gives them a different sort of appeal from other small pictures. Also the attractiveness of stamps themselves explains much of their popularity as a hobby.

It's fun to collect stamps

The urge to collect things is an instinctive part of human nature. Collecting—and there is no limit to the kinds of things collected—is fun. But of all the different collecting hobbies, collecting stamps has the most universal appeal. The exact number of collectors today is uncertain but informed estimates indicate that as many as 10% of

Stamp collecting appeals to every age group.

(Left) A young collector studies his album. (Right) Franklin D. Roosevelt, one of the most famous stamp collectors.

the American people are interested in stamps. Such enthusiasm is by no means limited to the United States. In European countries, especially, the proportion of collectors is even greater. In fact, with collectors all over the globe, stamp collecting is easily the world's most popular hobby.

Stamps offer a welcome change from the routine of business or school work. Collecting can fill odd moments or occupy many hours, but no matter how much time you can spare for your hobby, you will always wish you had just a little more! Time flies when you are involved in building up a collection—searching for stamps; sorting and identifying new acquisitions; arranging and mounting them in your album; studying reference books and catalogues to learn about each one. And, of course, there is the fun of meeting fellow collectors, swapping duplicates, and talking about your favorite stamps.

It's easy to collect stamps

One of the most enticing aspects of the hobby is the ease of getting started. If you have access to enough incoming mail, especially mail of a firm doing business abroad, you can build a collection without

All of the above stamps were taken from incoming mail. You can see how easy it is to gather an attractive stamp display without spending a cent.

spending a cent. Nearly everyone, however, progresses to the stage of spending at least nickels, dimes and quarters for stamps. There are literally thousands of stamps that can be bought for a penny a piece or less. These "penny stamps" include plenty of the older issues too! Spending can easily be kept within bounds and a modest budget won't keep you from enjoying this hobby. Many boys and girls enjoy stamp collecting within the limits of their weekly allowance.

Not much equipment is needed—only an album to house your collection, some hinges to attach your stamps to the pages, and a pair of stamp tongs to handle them with.

Stamps and these accessories can be purchased easily. Nearly every city has a professional stamp dealer; department and variety stores have sections devoted to the needs of collectors. Thousands operate exclusively by mail so you can be served no matter where you live without going beyond the mailbox at your front door. They will gladly let you see stamps "on approval," selections sent to you at home for your consideration. You are expected to return the stamps within ten days along with payment for any you keep. You can return the whole lot if nothing interests you, or if you think the price is too high; you are not under any obligation to buy.

Stamps have value

Few new collectors can resist asking about the monetary value of stamps. Newspaper articles about the discovery of rare varieties or errors mention values as high as half a million dollars for a sheet of stamps. Stamps of great value are the exception rather than the rule. Every stamp, though, does have a recognized, readily established value. This aspect of stamp collecting sets it apart from many other hobbies.

Stamps can be enjoyed over the years and yet if the day ever comes when a collector tires of his hobby, he is sure of getting back at least part of the money he put into it. If he has purchased wisely he can sometimes even realize a profit.

Fun and knowledge are the dividends you should expect to earn from collecting and studying stamps. Knowledge is valuable and you can certainly learn a lot from your stamps. Even so, one of the real thrills of collecting is to stumble across a stamp with a value greater than its cost—even if it is a stamp worth 50c. found in a packet of "penny approvals." Luck of course is a factor in coming across a valuable stamp, but recognizing a "find" depends upon your having a thorough knowledge of stamps. Every collector feels that some day his turn will come and he is always on the lookout for a good bargain, the unrecognized rarity or a great find.

Tips for the beginner

The best advice for the would-be collector is to start right in and collect all the stamps that come your way—nearly everyone starts "collecting" by trying to accumulate as many postage stamps as possible. This book will give you useful information about identifying, mounting and arranging stamps. It will give you valuable tips about buying and selling stamps.

Since there are now over one million varieties of stamps, you will soon realize that serious collecting will have to be limited to some workable project. Here you can read about the methods others have used to organize their stamps and about the kinds of collections they have built.

Whatever you decide to collect, study each stamp you get. Later, as you look through your album, you will delight in seeing and knowing the story of each of your possessions. There is a great deal of satisfaction in building a collection; in seeing it grow, stamp by stamp. There is a satisfying feeling of accomplishment in knowing that you have done the acquiring, sorting and mounting yourself and, of course, you can take pride in displaying your work.

A stamp collection can be a long-term project shared by every member of the family. Many of today's adult collectors began as youngsters. Stamps have a lasting interest and become more precious to their owner as he becomes familiar with each one. You will like collecting from the start, but your enjoyment will grow as you gain knowledge and experience along the way.

2. Before You Begin

Stamp collectors are sometimes called philatelists. The formal term for collecting is philately. All of philately focuses about these little pieces of paper called postage stamps. Before you begin, take a closer look at the stamps themselves.

On the surface

When you look at an assortment of stamps the first thing you notice is that every color imaginable has been represented. Collectors have given names to hundreds of colors, shades and hues. Of the variety of shapes and sizes, the vertical rectangle is commonest,

but you can also find almost as many horizontal rectangles, plus squares, triangles, diamonds, even an octagon and an isosceles trapezoid!

The largest stamp ever issued is the 1913 four-part express delivery stamp of China, which measures 9¾ by 2¾ inches (covering about 20 square inches). The smallest is an 1863 stamp of the Colombian state of Bolivar which measures 5/16 by 3/8 inch (covering only about ⅛ of a square inch). [From the *Guinness Book of World Records*.]

Stamps come in many sizes. (Left) Reproduction of a Japanese print by Sharaku. (Right) Reduced size South African wartime issues.

The picture portion of a stamp is called the "vignette." On most issues, the vignette is enclosed within a frame. On many modern issues, the picture covers the whole stamp. Stamps are often used on international mail, so the name or some device indicating the country of origin appears, except on the stamps of Great Britain.

The national name has never appeared on English stamps, presumably because Britain was the first nation to use stamps (beginning in 1840) and there was no need to differentiate them from stamps of other countries.

The first function of a stamp is to indicate the prepayment of a fee to the postal clerks so, of course, there must be an indication of its value.

The "margin" is the unprinted area outside the border of the design. As you will learn, collectors value accurately centered stamps with equal margins. Most stamps have a series of "teeth" or "holes" along the edge. These "perforations" allow the stamps to be separated easily. Some countries use a series of slits between

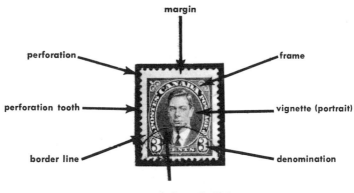

margin

perforation

frame

perforation tooth

vignette (portrait)

border line

denomination

postmark (cancellation)

The arrows show the principal features of a typical stamp.

stamps rather than punched holes, and such stamps are referred to as "roulette." No means of separation was provided for the earliest stamps and they had to be cut from the sheet with scissors. There are still occasional issues of "imperforate" stamps, without roulettes or perforations between them.

As mail passes through the post office, stamps are "cancelled," that is, invalidated to prevent their reuse. These cancellations are usually in the form of wavy ink lines or postmarks showing the name of the city where the cancellation was applied. Beginners generally get used stamps for their collection; cancelled stamps no longer have face value and cost less than "mint" or unused stamps. In many ways, used stamps are more interesting; you can be sure they have fulfilled their purpose of carrying mail and the cancellation usually shows when and where they were posted. On the other hand, a heavy cancellation interferes with the full appreciation of a stamp as a work of art.

Many of the stamps illustrated in this book are used stamps. To show the kinds of stamps that are readily available to beginners, nearly all of the stamps illustrated are inexpensive varieties that you can collect easily or purchase from any dealer at low cost.

On the other side

When you become an experienced collector you will often refer to the back side of a stamp for information. Two stamps are not necessarily identical just because they look alike on the surface. The back side of a stamp will tell you about the kind of paper it is printed on, whether the paper was watermarked and, if it is an unused stamp, you can see the gum. In judging the condition of a stamp you will soon find it very important to check the back side for thin spots and old hinges.

The beginner is usually not concerned with these minor variations. Many collectors never do bother with anything more than "face-different" stamps. There are some technical things beyond the scope of this book and of most collectors. In the chapter on advanced collecting you will learn how to recognize and identify watermark varieties. When you first take up the hobby, however, it is enough to know that if you have the time and inclination really to study and examine your stamps there can be more to collecting than getting one of each kind and putting it in an album.

Different kinds of stamps

Part of the fun of collecting is getting acquainted with the different types of stamps.

A postage stamp represents the promise of a government to perform a certain postal service, but the modern postal system provides a variety of services and sometimes different stamps are used for each one. Many stamp catalogues and albums have separate listings for each group of stamps so you will have to learn to recognize the various classifications:

GENERAL ISSUES. General issues are stamps that can be used for regular mail or any other service. In the United States, for example, general issues may be used for regular mail or a service, such as special delivery, even though there are distinctive special delivery stamps. (Special delivery stamps, however, cannot be used for regular service.)

(Left) An early biplane shown on a 1919 German airmail stamp. (Right) This recent stamp from Israel shows a modern jet transport.

AIRMAIL. The design of airmail stamps usually has wings or an airplane or some other symbol of flying. Special stamps that are readily identified for airpost service speed the dispatching of mail to the airport.

SPECIAL DELIVERY. These stamps show payment of the fee for the special service of having a letter taken from the receiving post office straight to its destination by a postal messenger ahead of the regular delivering postman.

The amount to be collected is the prominent feature of most postage due stamps.

POSTAGE DUE. Stamps in this class are used on letters or parcels which were mailed without sufficient postage, or are being returned to the sender because of a faulty address, refusal to accept, or some similar reason. They show the postman how much he must collect before handing over the item.

In addition, you will occasionally come across stamps for other special services such as parcel post, registered or certified mail, special handling for parcel post, newspaper stamps, and pneumatic post stamps from Italy for letters sent through underground tubes.

The basic stamp issue of a country is called the "definitive issue." The definitives include a wide enough range of denomination to prepay the lowest unit rate or the highest. The stamps are usually of convenient size and are intended for use over an unspecified period of time. They are available concurrently with special commemorative or semi-postal issues. Temporary issues of stamps

(Left) Two-centavo stamp of the 1928 Guatemala definitive issue. (Center) UN CEN-TAVO surcharge reducing the value of the stamp to fill a need for the lower denomination. (Right) A bisected half of the two-centavo value used provisionally as a one-centavo stamp.

placed in use pending completion of a regular issue are called "provisionals." Commemorative stamps, on the other hand, are issued in limited numbers and, when sold out, are seldom reprinted. They have pictures and inscriptions calling attention to the person or event being commemorated and are usually larger than normal stamps to allow more area for the design. The beauty and historic

The U.S. Dag Hammarskjold memorial stamp received world-wide publicity because of an unusual color error. (Left) Yellow color plate inverted—note color in left and right margins, white area around building. (Right) Normal stamp.

significance of commemoratives often create an interest among people who are otherwise indifferent to stamps.

Semi-postal stamps provide a government-supported means of raising money for worthy projects. Semi-postals are sold to the public through post offices for more than their postal value; the difference is turned over to the selected cause. Semi-postal stamps are imprinted with both values—the amount for valid prepayment of postage and the surtax the purchaser pays. After a specified time

Semi-postal stamps with surtaxes for tuberculosis fund, Red Cross and child health. The black border shows mourning for Queen Astrid, killed in an auto accident.

these stamps are declared obsolete for postal use. The public can still buy regular stamps for their mail at no premium, but semi-postal designs are particularly handsome to encourage their use. Funds raised are usually for child-welfare, the Red Cross or other organizations of undoubted merit. Issues like the French stamps for unemployed intellectuals may be open to question. The United States and Great Britain are two countries that have never used semi-postals.

Overprinted Stamps

In every assortment of stamps you will find some that have an "overprint," not a cancellation but a mark, inscription or design on the face that was not part of the original design. These overprints are especially interesting because they alter the value, use or locality of the stamp to fill a temporary need. Others may show a lost war

(Left) Commemorative overprint produced on short notice. (Center and right) Surcharges changing the postal value.

or a change in government. A few overprints commemorate an occasion or a person and were probably made because there was not time to design and print a regular commemorative stamp. Most overprints are to change the value of a stamp; this kind of special overprint is called a "surcharge." Collectors, of course, consider an overprinted stamp completely different from the original stamp without the overprint.

Stamps overprinted to limit their use to official mail. The stamp at the right was further restricted to official army business.

In many countries, "official" stamps used on government business are overprinted with that word to prevent unauthorized use. They are usually for general use of all branches of government but sometimes "departmental" stamps are overprinted with the name of a department for the exclusive use of that particular department.

When a foreign army moves into captured territory, "occupation

stamps" may be issued for use in the conquered territory. Some nations produce whole new issues for occupational use, but more often stamps of the victorious nation are overprinted for use in the conquered area. Collectors can follow the fortunes of war by studying their stamps.

City names overprinted on the face of U.S. stamps do not alter the use of the stamps. These are "precancelled" stamps which have been invalidated before being applied to mail. They are used only under permit by large firms to save a step in processing their mail. Canada, France and Belgium are other countries using precancelled stamps.

Air raid propaganda overprint on Chinese airmail stamp issued during the final days of Japanese occupation.

Every stamp has a story behind it. Not only does the stamp face indicate the intended use (sometimes the date), and the circumstances of its issue, but there is a story told by the design; you can learn why it was chosen and a little about the people and places pictured.

3. Getting Started

In starting your collection, the first thing is to get some stamps. You may be able to accumulate an assortment from incoming mail or with luck, you may have a collecting friend who will give you some of his duplicates. Otherwise, you will have to buy your first stamps.

General collecting

Nearly everyone starts with a general collection—stamps of all kinds from all countries. This is the best way, as beginners should get acquainted with all kinds of stamps, not just a particular kind. Besides, it is the least expensive way to begin—you get the most stamps for the least money. Later on you may want to limit your collecting, but don't be in a hurry to specialize. Take enough time to find out what stamps really interest you. Plunging right in on a specialized collection without some general experience may result in an unfortunate choice, and you will spend time and money on a project only to find that you really have no interest in finishing it. A general collection lets you preview the possibilities for specialization and provides the basic stamp knowledge a collector needs to build a worthwhile advanced collection.

Mixtures and packets

Mixtures and packets are for sale in all kinds of places; department and variety stores, hobby shops and, of course, there are stamp dealers and shows all over the world. Stamp dealers are collectors at heart and have put in lots of time studying stamps. They can be very helpful to you in getting started. At the stamp store you will find stamps for sale in mixtures and packets, used and unused sets, even individual stamps of every description. A few sets and a handful of single stamps are not much of a start; you will be more interested in buying a worldwide assortment. Handling costs are much lower on assortments than on single stamps so you will get many more stamps for your money.

Stamp mixtures and packets
give the greatest number of
stamps for the least cost.

There are two kinds of world-wide assortments, "mixtures" and "all-different packets." Mixtures are just that, a supposedly unpicked and unsorted combination of stamps from a variety of sources. They contain many duplicates. You will be fortunate to get 200 different stamps from a mixture of 500, but the packet is very inexpensive, nevertheless. A worldwide mixture of 1,000 stamps costs about $2.00. Most of the stamps in a mixture are "on paper," still stuck to a corner of the original envelope.

The best investment for a new collector is an all-different packet. You will only mount one copy of a stamp in an album and you can use every stamp in an all-different packet. Duplicates do have value as trading material, but it is best to avoid the unnecessary accumulation of duplicates this early in collecting. There will be enough time later when they can't be avoided. All-different packets are not expensive either. A packet of 1,000 all-different stamps costs about $5.00. Packet prices vary somewhat depending upon how many countries are represented in the assortment, how many pictorials, high values and "mint (unused)" stamps they contain. Nearly all of the stamps in packets are "off paper."

How big?

Packets come in sizes ranging from 100 to 50,000 different. The price per stamp goes up in proportion to the size of the packet. A packet of 10,000 different costs four times as much as two packets of 5,000 different. A packet of 5,000 contains the commonest stamps of a wide range of countries. Scarcer stamps of the same countries have to be added to the original 5,000 to make the bigger packet. The second 5,000 cost about three times as much as the first 5,000.

Don't be too ambitious at first. You want enough stamps to have an interesting variety, but not more than you can handle or absorb. Boys and girls should start with a packet of 2,000 or 3,000 different ($12.50–20.00). Adults will probably want 3,000 to 5,000 different ($20.00–50.00). If you get more than that, the stamps will be difficult to identify and sort (unless you buy them already sorted and mounted in booklets, but that takes away the fun of working with them yourself).

If you decide to start with 2,000 different, buy that size right away. It won't work to buy a packet of 1,000 now and 1,000 later, because they will contain just about the same assortment. Starting with a packet that is too large on the other hand, will result in many duplicates later when you begin building up your collection with packets from individual countries.

Buying an album

Having purchased or decided upon some stamps, you will next need an album for mounting them. There are two "musts" in choosing your album—get one that is printed, and be sure it is loose-leaf. Printed albums are arranged by country and many of the spaces have illustrations that are useful for identifying stamps and serve as guides for mounting them on the pages. With a loose-

leaf album you can always add pages to take care of new issues or other stamps for which no space is provided. Some manufacturers publish periodic supplements that can be inserted in their albums to provide spaces for recently issued stamps.

Transferring a collection of even a few thousand stamps from one album to another is a big job, so buy one right away that is large enough to insure your not outgrowing it too soon. Adding extra pages to a loose-leaf album will take care of some overflow, but you won't like having more stamps on blank pages than in the printed spaces. Albums are made to accommodate anywhere from about 3,000 to nearly 100,000 stamps. To determine what size is best for you, estimate how many stamps you think you will get in the next 3 or 4 years. No album will provide spaces for just exactly the stamps you will get, so make some allowance for that. A rule of thumb is to buy an album that has spaces for about twice the number of stamps you expect to have.

Albums with fewer than 6,000 spaces are only for the youngest collectors, probably someone who is "helping dad" with his collection. Fewer than 5% of the stamps issued can be accommodated in an album this small, so no matter how modestly you collect, you will get too many stamps for which there are no spaces.

Boys and girls who are serious about collecting will find an album with 10,000 to 20,000 spaces just about right. This size should

Albums of this type provide spaces for about 20,000 stamps.

provide enough spaces to hold all of the stamps you are likely to accumulate for quite a while although, if you spend $1 a week on stamps, you will need a bigger album in 3 or 4 years. Enough stamps are illustrated for you to identify what you have and to guide you in making orderly arrangements on the pages. Remember that only stamps issued before the album was printed are illustrated, so get one that has been revised within the past year or two and be sure to buy the loose-leaf edition so you can add blank pages for new stamps. This size album will cost about $10.00 to $15.00.

The albums pictured above are suitable for a somewhat larger collection, providing an average of 35,000 spaces.

Adult collectors generally start with a bigger album. The next group has about 25,000 to 40,000 spaces. This sounds like a lot of stamps when you are just starting out, but if you spend $3-5 a week on stamps for the next 3 years you can build a collection of 20,000 different. A great proportion of the stamps you will get will be illustrated in larger albums, and there are likely to be spaces for all but the rare early issues, high values and minor varieties. Even though you later limit your collecting to some special field, you will probably maintain an interest in your general collection. You will have to pay from $15.00 to $20.00 for albums in this group.

Still larger albums are available — the very biggest having spaces for nearly every stamp issued. Besides face-different stamps, they accommodate perforation, watermark, paper and minor design varieties. Just as you must be sure to get an album large enough for

These albums are designed for the advanced collector, with spaces for over 75,000 stamps.

your needs, you should also beware of buying one that is too big for a beginner. Five or even 10 thousand stamps get lost in a set of albums with 100,000 spaces. The biggest albums should be a second purchase made only after you have been collecting for a while and gone as far as you can with a smaller album. An experienced collector who is seriously maintaining a world-wide, general collection must have a large, comprehensive album. Albums for 75,000 or more stamps range in price from $50 to $100.

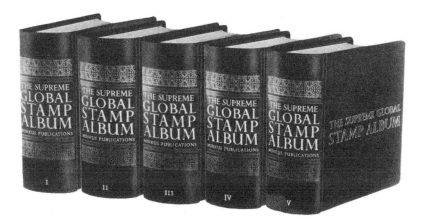

The multi-volume Minkus Supreme Global album provides spaces for approximately 200,000 stamps arranged in alphabetical order by country name.

The multi-part Scott International Postage Stamp album provides a space for nearly every stamp ever issued. The volumes are chronologically arranged. As a measure of the pace of new releases, Part I houses a century of issues from 1840 to 1940 while Part XIV contains only stamps from the year 1978. The entire series through 1985 now consists of 24 volumes.

Stamp hinges

The only sensible way for a beginner to mount stamps is with "stamp hinges." Hinges are small pieces of semitransparent paper coated with special peelable gum. You can peel them off the back of your stamps without damaging the paper.

You can buy hinges prefolded (which save time) or flat in packages of 1,000 for about $1.00. If you buy them flat, fold the hinge a third of the way down with the gummed side out. Moisten the short side with the tip of your tongue and attach it to the back of the stamp. The fold goes toward the top of the stamp just below the row of perforations. Next, moisten the bottom half of the long side of the hinge and place the stamp in the proper space in your album.

The drawing at the left shows a hinge properly attached to the back of a stamp. Be especially careful not to moisten the gum on the back of unused stamps or you will find them sticking to your album page when you want to remove them.

For a neat looking job, take care to place the stamp squarely in its space. If you are working with unused stamps be careful not to moisten the stamp's gum before or when you put it in the album or you may find it will stick to the page when you try to take it out again. A special warning—never try to remove a hinge from the back of a stamp while it is still damp. Hinges aren't "peelable" until the gum is completely dry.

If you find pieces of old hinges on the back of a stamp, be sure to remove them before you attach the new one. Too many layers of hinges make a stamp bulge when it lies in an album under the weight of other pages.

Stamp tongs

Picking a stamp up with your fingers is often awkward. You can handle stamps easily and safely, though, with a pair of tongs, which are like household tweezers except they have flat blades at the end; these let you get a firm grip on a stamp without tearing it.

This Czechoslovakian stamp illustrates the proper use of stamp tongs.

With your tongs you can hold the stamp straight as you place it on the page. Also, you are less likely to soil or crease it. A pair of tongs costs only $2.00 to $3.00.

Interleaving

To pack in as many stamps as possible, an album must be designed with spaces for mounting stamps on both sides of each page. As the album fills up, stamps mounted on facing pages sometimes catch and pull out as the pages are turned. Putting glassine or acetate interleaving between the pages will prevent this. Glassine interleaves cost about 10c. each, acetate 15c. Albums bulge a bit as your collection grows, but extra binders are usually available. If your album becomes too full, you can get an extra binder and divide the pages.

The Scott Standard Postage Stamp Catalogue, a four-volume annual publication giving date of issue, design, denomination, color, surcharge or overprint, perforation and watermark, with illustration or description of designs and prices of most stamps. Volume I: U.S. and its Possessions, U.N. and British Commonwealth of Nations. Volume II: World Nations, A through F. Volume III: World Nations, G through O. Volume IV: World Nations, P through Z.

Catalogues

World-wide catalogues give listings and illustrations, by country, of every recognized variety of stamp. With a catalogue you can verify the identification of a stamp, determine its date of issue and find the value of used and unused copies. If you buy a catalogue, it should be the Scott or the Minkus, both published in the U.S. Albums published in the U.S. are designed after them, dealers' ads use their numbers, stamp newspapers and magazines base their articles and stories on them. The prices listed in catalogues are

Minkus Publications, Inc. suspended producing their annual three-volume New World-Wide Postage Stamp Catalog after 1981, then began publishing a series of regional and single-country catalogues. These handy smaller-sized catalogues, which are priced from $4.75 to $9.95 each, have proven to be extremely popular with collectors.

intended merely as guides. The market value of a stamp is often less than its catalogue value, often in the neighborhood of 60-75% of the figure shown. No stamp is valued at less than 5c. An up-to-date catalogue costs $45-70. Contrary to suggestions often given, it is not essential for a beginner to have a catalogue. While it is a most useful tool, it is a substantial investment that you can defer for a while, since you can make do by using your album pages for information and using free dealers' price lists for values.

4. Working with Stamps

Stamps still on paper from mixtures or on envelopes that come in the mail must be soaked off before you can do anything further with them. Don't make the mistake of pulling them off because you will surely tear them or create a thin spot in the paper. Soaking the pieces in cool water for about 15 minutes will loosen the gum enough for you to slide the stamps right off the scraps of paper.

Stamps are usually soaked off paper before they go into an album. You may want to save the full postmarks sometimes though, as they often tell when and where the stamp was used.

Dry the stamps by putting them face down on a clean blotter or other absorbent paper. If they curl up as they dry, press them in a heavy book overnight to flatten them out again. Be careful to hold the stamps flat as you close the book on them. If a corner of a stamp gets turned under, it will be permanently creased. Stamps stuck to pieces of colored paper should be soaked apart from the others, because the color can run and stain the other stamps.

Sorting stamps

When all of your stamps are "off paper" you are ready to start sorting them out. This is your first chance to look at them individually, to see what you have, and begin arranging them for mounting in your album. A large table is a good place to work; you need plenty of room to spread your stamps out and the family can gather around and enjoy the fun too. Separating them by country is the first and most difficult step toward turning an accumulation of stamps into an orderly collection.

You will have to separate them in stages if you have any quantity at all to sort, since an assortment of 2,000 stamps can easily represent

150 or more different stamp-issuing nations and colonies. It's impossible to make individual piles for each country the first time through. Make your first division according to the alphabet, A B C, etc. Of course you will have to make an extra pile at one side for the stamps whose country of origin you don't know. The first few times you sort stamps, this will probably become the biggest pile of all.

Once the assortment is broken down into smaller groups, take them one at a time and separate the stamps by country. Have a supply of plain envelopes on hand and label one for each country. You can use the same envelopes later for storing duplicates. One sitting is seldom enough to finish a sorting job, but with envelopes handy it is easy to pick up your work and keep it in order until next time.

Identifying stamps

After all the stamps you can recognize are sorted into envelopes by country you can turn your attention to that pile of stamps you haven't identified. Most stamps are easy to attribute; the only problem is knowing what to look for. Because there are a great many British colonial issues, a sizable proportion of the world's stamps show the name of the issuing country in English.

These stamps show the names of the issuing countries in English even though English is not their native language.

Then, too, many countries are known in English by the same name as their native languages. In most of the nations of Central and South America, Spanish is the official language but you will recognize the stamps of Argentina, Bolivia, Chile, Colombia, Cuba, Ecuador, Guatemala, Honduras, Mexico, Nicaragua, Panama, Paraguay, Peru, El Salvador, Uruguay, Venezuela and others right away because we use their Spanish names when we speak and write English. The same is true too of some other countries that use languages besides Spanish.

The names of several countries are exactly the same in English as in their native language which makes identification easy.

Another large group of countries issue stamps on which the name of the country in the native language is similar enough to what we call them in English for you to guess where they are from. Here are some foreign names that you will recognize: Belgique (Belgium), Brasil (Brazil), Ceskoslovenska (Czechoslovakia), Eire (Ireland), Republique Francaise (France), Norge (Norway), Polska (Poland), Espana (Spain), Sverige (Sweden).

If the name of the country doesn't appear in English, it is often so similar that a collector can easily guess where a stamp is from. (Left) Norway, (center) Czechoslovakia, (right) Poland.

Other countries issue stamps that are not so easily identified. You may need help to know that "Deutsches Reich" is Germany and that "Helvetia" is Switzerland and it's almost certain that you won't recognize "ΠOYTA" on Russian stamps or "CPbNJA" as Serbia. A few stamps like these do not have lettering or identifying elements that can even be expressed in English characters. Before you can put these stamps in your album you will have to do a little detective work to find out what country they are from. First, read through the table of contents or index of your album to acquaint yourself at least slightly with the names of the past and present stamp-issuing countries of the world.

Then, study the design and wording of your unknown stamps for clues to their identity. When you have more experience with stamps, you will recognize most of them on sight from key words or familiar characteristics of the design. Check first of all to see whether the name of the country appears anywhere in English. For example, a stamp with the inscription AFRIQUE OCCIDENTAL GABON is from the former French West African country, Gabon. You may not have known before that Gabon was a stamp-issuing territory, but seeing the name on the stamp in a position following the other words (which appear on many stamps) can be the clue you need. You can still make the identification by looking for the whole inscription, AFRIQUE EQUATORIALE GABON in the following list where you will be referred to Gabon.

Gabon

Fiume

Be careful not to pass over the name of some small country printed plainly on the face of a stamp without realizing it is the very thing you are trying to uncover. Most people have never heard of Fiume, for example, yet it had its own postage stamps for a few years and there are spaces for them in your album. FIUME appears clearly on its stamps.

Whenever you tentatively identify a stamp and want to verify your hunch, turn to the page in your album for the country in question and compare the stamp with those illustrated. Look at all of the stamps from the country; there may be separate sections for Post Offices Abroad, Occupation Stamps, etc. If you are right, you should find either an exact picture or one similar enough to convince you that your attribution is correct. Don't mount the stamp in your album just yet though. Even if you find a picture of the exact stamp it is best to wait until you have all of your stamps sorted. You may find that you have more than one copy of the same stamp, in which case you should select the one in best condition for your album.

If looking at the inscription on a stamp doesn't tell you what country it is from, you will have to find the key word or element in the following table. Pick the word that looks the most promising and look it up. If you find it listed, the table will tell you where to find the stamp in your album. Turn to the page for the country as directed and compare the stamp with the pictures until you find the exact stamp or one very similar. If the word you choose isn't listed, keep trying until you find one that is. Generally speaking, words such as "republic, airmail, postage, cent" and their foreign equivalents are not listed because these are not names of countries and, therefore, are not useful in identification. Words that seem unusual on a stamp are likely to be the distinctive key words. Check any overprints first since they may change the country under whose heading they are to be mounted in your album. If there aren't spaces in the album and the overprint is not in the following list, then you can assume it doesn't change the country and you can go on to using the words in the original design for identifying the stamp.

The visual identification section following the key word listing will help you identify stamps without recognizable words. Compare your stamps with the illustrations and watch especially for the key element of the design shown in the picture. The word and picture sections have been worked out so that nearly every stamp can be correctly identified. Even so, you may wind up with a few stamps that you can't seem to locate. If this happens, keep them handy as you put stamps in your album and watch for their pictures as you go.

GUIDE TO STAMP IDENTIFICATION

A.B. (overprint on Russian stamps)—Far Eastern Republic.

ACObHbI ATPAA—White Russia.

ACORES—Azores.

A. E. F.—French Equatorial Africa.

AFGHAN, AFGHANES—Afghanistan.

AFRICA OCCIDENTAL ESPANOLA—Spanish West Africa.

AFRICA ORIENTALE ITALIANA—Italian East Africa.

AFRIQUE EQUATORIALE AFRICA— French Equatorial Africa.

AFRIQUE EQUATORIALE GABON—Gabon.

AFRIQUE OCCIDENTAL FRANCAISE— French West Africa.

ALAOUITES (overprint on stamps of France and Syria).

ALBANIA (overprint on stamps of Italy)—Italy, Offices in Turkey.

ALEXANDRIE—France, Officers in Egypt.

ALGERIE—Algeria.

ALLEMAGNE DUITSCHLAND (overprint on stamps of Belgium)—Belgian occupation of Germany.

ALWAR—India, native state.

A.M.G. - F.T.T., A.M.G. - V.G. (overprint on stamps of Italy)—Italy, Allied occupation.

A M POST—Allied Military Government in Germany.

AMTLICHER VERKEHR—Wurttemberg.

ANDORRE (overprint on stamps of France)— Andorra.

ANTIOQUIA—Colombia.

 APAXMAI—Greece.

A PAYER TE BETALEN—Belgium.

APURIMAC—Peru.

A. R. Colon (overprint on stamps of Colombia)— Panama, under Colombian dominion.

ASSISTENCIA - D. L. No. 72 (overprint on stamps of Portuguese India)—Timor.

A & T (overprint on stamps of France)—Annam and Tonkin, French Indo-China.

AUNIS (overprint on stamps of Finland)—Russia, under Finnish occupation.
AVION MESSRE TAFARI—Abyssinia.
AVISPORTO—Denmark.
AYACUCHO—Peru.
AYTONOMOE—Epirus.
AZERBAIDJAN, AZERBAYEDJAN—Azerbaijan.

BADEN—Germany (French occupation).
B.A. ERITREA (overprint on stamps of Great Britain)—Great Britain, Offices in Eritrea.
BAGHDAD (overprint on stamps of Turkey)—Mesopotamia, British occupation.
BAHA—India - Bamra, native state.
BAHAWALPUR—Pakistan.
BAHRAIN—India, native state.
BAMRA—India, native state.
BANI (overprint on Austrian stamps)—Austrian occupation of Roumania.
BARANYA (overprint on stamps of Hungary)—Hungary under Serbian occupation.

BARCELONA—Spain.
BARWANI—India, native state.
BASEL—Switzerland.
B.A. SOMALIA (overprint on stamps of Great Britain)—Great Britain, for use in Somalia.
BATAAN & CORREGIDOR—Phillippines, under Japanese occupation.
B. A. TRIPOLITANA (overprint on stamps of Great Britain)—Great Britain, for use in Tripolitania.
BATYM—Batum.
BAYERN, BAYR—Bavaria.

B. C. A. (overprint on stamps of Rhodesia)—British Central Africa.
B.C.O.F. - JAPAN - 1946 (overprint on stamps of Australia)—Australia, military forces in Japan.
BEHAEHCKAR—Russia (Wenden).
BELGIE, BELGIQUE—Belgium.
BELGIEN (overprint on German stamps)—German occupation of Belgium.
BELGISCH CONGO—Belgian Congo.
BENADIR—Italian Somaliland.
BENGASI (overprint on stamps of Italy)—Italy, Offices in Tripoli.

BERLIN (overprint for use in American, British
and French occupation sectors of Berlin)—
Germany.

BEYROUTH (overprint on Russian stamps)—
Russia, Offices in Turkey.

BHOPAL—India, native state.

BHOR—India, native state.

BIJAWAR—India, native state.

B.M.A. ERITREA (overprint on stamps of Great
Britain)—Great Britain, Offices in Eritrea.

B.M.A. SOMALIA (overprint on stamps of
Great Britain)—Great Britain, for use in
Somalia.

B.M.A. TRIPOLITANIA (overprint on stamps
of Great Britain)—Great Britain, for use in
Tripolitania.

B. N. F. CASTELLORIZO—Castellorizo.

BOGCHAH, BOGACHES—Yemen.

BOHMEN UND MAHREN—Czechoslovakia —
Bohemia and Moravia.

BOLIVAR—Colombia.

BOLLA DELLA POSTA DI SICILIA—Two
Sicilies.

BOLLA DELLA POSTA NAPOLETANA—Two
Sicilies.

BOSNIEN-HERZEGOVINA—Bosnia and
Herzegovina.

BOYACA—Colombia.

BRASIL—Brazil.

BRAUNSCHWEIG—Brunswick, German state.

BRIEFPOST—Germany (French occupation).

BRITISH EAST AFRICA COMPANY (overprint on stamps of Great Britain)—British East
Africa.

BRITISH NEW GUINEA—Now Papua.

BRITISH OCCUPATION (overprint)—Batum.

BRITISH SOUTH AFRICA COMPANY—
Rhodesia.

BRUNEI (overprint on the stamps of Labuan)—
Brunei.

BUENOS AIRES—Argentina.

BULGARIE—Bulgaria.

BUNDESPOST—German Federal Republic.

BUNDI—India, native state.

BURMA (overprint on stamps of India)—Burma.

BUSSAHIR—India, native state.

CABO JUBY—Cape Juby.

CABO VERDE—Cape Verde.

CAHATOPyMb—Bulgaria.

CALCHI (overprint on stamps of Italy)—Italy, Aegean Islands.

CALINO (overprint on stamps of Italy)—Italy - Aegean Islands.

CALLAO (overprint on stamps of Chile)—Peru, under Chilean occupation.

CAMB AUST. SIGILLUM NOV.—New South Wales.

CAMBODGE—Cambodia.

CAMBODIA—French Indo-China.

CAMEROUN—Cameroons.

CAMPECHE—Mexico.

CAMPIONE D'ITALIA—Italian enclave within borders of Switzerland.

CANTON (overprint on stamps of Indo-China)—France, Offices in China.

CARCHI (overprint on Italian stamps)—Italy - Aegean Islands.

CASO (overprint on stamps of Italy)—Italy - Aegean Islands.

CASTELLORISO, CASTELROSSO—Castellorizo.

CAUCA—Colombia.

CAVALLE (overprint on stamps of France)—France, Offices in Turkey.

C C C P (Union of Socialist Soviet Republics)—Russia.

C. CH. (overprint on French Colonies)—Cochin China.

CECHY A MORAVA—Czechoslovakia - (Bohemia and Moravia).

C. E. F. (Cameroon Expeditionary Force)—Cameroon, on German stamps of Kamerun.

CENTENAIRE DU GABON—French Equatorial Africa.

CENTIMOS (with no country name)—Spain.

CESKOSLOVENSKO—Czechoslovakia.

C. G. H. S. (overprint on Prussian stamps)—Upper Silesia.

CHALA—Peru.

CHAMBA STATE—India, native state.

CHARKHARI—India, native state.

CHEMINS DE FER SPOORWEGEN—Belgium.

CHIFFRE TAXE (without country name)—
France (on perforated stamps)—French Colonies (on imperforate stamps).

CHINA (overprint on stamps of Hong Kong)—
Great Britain, Offices in China.

CHINA (overprint on stamps of Germany)—
Germany, Offices in China.

CHINE (overprint on stamps of France and Indo-China)—France, Offices in China.

C. I. H. S. (on stamps of Germany)—Upper Silesia.

CILICIE—Cilicia.

CIRENAICA—Cyrenaica.

COCHIN—India, native state.

COLIS POSTAL—Belgium.

COLONIES DE L'EMPIRE FRANCAISE—French Colonies.

COLONIES POSTES (on regular issue for all colonies)—French Colonies.

COMUNICACIONES—Spain.

COMORES—Comoro Islands.

CONGO BELGE—Belgian Congo.

CONGO FRANCAIS (overprint in French Colonies)—French Congo.

CONGO FRANCAIS GABON—Gabon.

CONSTANTINOPLE (overprint on stamps of Russia)—Russia, Offices in Turkey.

CONSTANTINOPLI (overprint on stamps of Italy)—Italy, Offices in Turkey.

COO (overprint on stamps of Italy)—Italy - Aegean Islands.

CORDOBA—Argentina.

COREA—Korea.

CORFU (overprint on stamps of Italy and Greece)—Corfu.

CORREIO (with no country name and denominations in "Reis")—Portugal.

CORREO CHANADINA—Colombia.

CORREO ESPANOL MARRUECOS—Spain, Offices in Morocco.

CORREO ESPANOL TANGER—Spain.

CORREOS Y TELEGs—Spain.

CORREO URGENTE—Spain.

CORRIENTES—Argentina.

COSTA ATLANTICA—Nicaragua.

COTE D'IVOIRE—Ivory Coast.

COTE FRANCAIS DES SOMALIS—Somali Coast.
CPbNJA—Serbia.
CPNCKA—Serbia.
CTOTNHKN—Bulgaria.
CUBA (overprint on stamps of the United States) —Cuba, under U.S. Administration.
CUERNAVACA—Mexico.
CUNDINAMARCA—Colombia.
CURACAO—now Netherland Antilles.
CUZCO—Peru.
C. X. C.—Jugoslavia.

DANMARK—Denmark.
DANSK-VESTINDIEN—Danish West Indies.
DARDANELLES (overprint on stamps of Russia) —Russia, Offices in Turkey.
D. B. L. (on stamps of Far Eastern Rep.)— Siberia (with additional print in blue).
DEDEAGH—France, Offices in Turkey.
DEL GOLFO DE GUINEA—Spanish Guinea.
DEUTSCHE NEU-GUINEA—German New Guinea.
DEUTSCHE OSTAFRICA—German East Africa.
DEUTSCHE SUDWESTAFRIKA—German South-West Africa.
DEUTSCHE DEMOKRATISCHE REPUBLIK —Germany (Russian Zone).
DEUTSCHE FELDPOST—Germany.
DEUTSCHE POST—Germany, Allied occupation.
DEUTSCHES REICH—Germany.
DEUTSCHLAND—Germany, Allied occupation.
DEUTSCHOSTERREICH—Austria.
D'HAITI—Haiti.
DHAR—India, native state.
DISTRITO 18°—Peru.
DJ (overprint on stamps of Obock)—Somali Coast.
DJIBOUTI (overprint on stamps of Obock)— Somali Coast.
D. M. (overprint)—Danzig.
DOPLATA—Central Lithuania and Poland.

DOPLATNE—Czechoslovakia.

DRZAVA, DRZAVNA—Jugoslavia.

DUC. DI. PARMA—Parma.

DUITSCH OOST AFRIKA BELGISCHE BE-
ZETTING (overprint on stamps of Congo)—
Belgian East Africa, Belgian occupation.

DURAZZO (overprint on stamps of Italy)—
Italy, Offices in Turkey.

DUTTIA—India, native state.

D. V. R. (overprint on stamps of Russia)—Far
Eastern Republic.

E. A. (overprint on stamps of Greece)—Greece-
Chios, Aegean Islands.

EAST AFRICA and UGANDA PROTECTOR-
ATE—East Africa and Uganda or Kenya and
Uganda.

EAST INDIA POSTAGE—India. If overprint
with a crown and new values—Straits Settlements.

EDD (overprint)—Greece - Dodecanese Islands.

E. E. F.—Palestine, British military occupation.

EESTE, EESTI—Estonia.

EE. UU. DE C.—Colombia.

EGEO (overprint on stamps of Italy)—Italy -
Aegian Islands.

EGYPTE, EGYPTIENNES—Egypt.

EINZUZIEHEN—Danzig.

EIRE—Ireland.

EMPIRE FRANC, FRANCAISE—France or
French Colonies.

ENAPIOMON—Greece.

EONIKH—Greece.

EPMAKb—South Russia.

ESCUELAS—Venezuela.

ESPANA, ESPANOL—Spain.

ESTADO DA INDIA—Portuguese India.

EST AFRICAIN ALLEMAND OCCUPATION
BELGE (overprint on stamps of Congo with
new values)—Belgian East Africa (without
value)—German East Africa.

ESTENSI POST—Modena.

ESTERO (overprint on stamps of Italy)—Italy,
Offices in China.

ÉTABLISSEMENTS DANS L'INDE—French
India.

ÉTAT FRANCAIS—France.
ÉTAT IND. DU CONGO—Congo.
ETHIOPIE or ETHIOPIENNES—Ethiopia.
EUPEN & MALMEDY (overprint on stamps of
    Belgium)—Belgian occupation of Germany.

FACTAJ (overprint)—Roumania.
FARIDKOT—India, native state.
FDO. POO.—Fernando Po.
FEDERATED MALAY STATES—Straits Settle-
    ments.
FEN - FN—Manchukuo.
FEZZAN—Libya.
FILIPINAS—Philippines.
FIVME—Fiume.
FRANCE D'OUTRE-MER—General issue of
    French Colonies.
FRANCO BOLLO (without country name)
    perforated stamps—Italy, imperforate stamps—
    Sardinia.
FREI DURCH ABLOSUNG (NR 16)—Baden.
FREI DURCH ABLOSUNG (NR 21)—Prussia.
FREIMARKE (without country name)—Ger-
    many.
FREISTAAT BAYERN (overprint on stamps of
    Germany)—Bavaria.

G (overprint on Cape of Good Hope stamps)—
    Griqualand West.
GAB (overprint on stamps of French colonies)—
    Gabon.
GARCH—Nejd.
G. E. A. (overprint on stamps of East Africa and
    Uganda)—German East Africa.
G. E. A. (overprint on stamps of Kenya)—Tan-
    ganyika.
GENERAL GOUVERNEMENT—Poland (Ger-
    man occupation).
GENEVE—Switzerland.
GEORGIE - GEORGIENNE—Georgia.
GIBRALTAR (overprint on Bermuda stamps)—
    Gibraltar.
GILBERT and ELLICE PROTECTORATE
    (overprint on Fiji stamps)—Gilbert and Ellice
    Islands.

G. P. E. (overprint on French Colonies stamps)—
Guadeloupe.

GRAND LIBAN—Lebanon.

G. R. I. (overprint on stamps of German New
Guinea or Marshall Islands)—New Britain.

G. R. I. (overprint on stamps of German Samoa)
—Samoa.

GRONLAND—Greenland.

GROSSDEUTSCHES REICH—Germany.

GROSSDEUTSCHES REICH BOHMEN and
MAHREN—Czechoslovakia - Bohemia and
Moravia.

GROSSDEUTSCHES REICH GENERAL-
GOUVERNMENT—Poland (German occupation).

GUADALAJARA—Mexico.

GUANACASTE—Costa Rica.

GUINE—Guinea.

GUINEA CONTINENTAL—Spanish Guinea.

GUINEA CORREOS—Spanish Guinea.

GUINEA ESPANOLA—Spanish Guinea.

GUINEE FRANCAIS—French Guinea.

GUYANE FRANCAISE—French Guiana.

G. W. (overprint on stamps of Cape of Good Hope)
—Griqualand West.

GWALIOR—India, native state.

G & D (overprint on French colonies stamps)—
Guadeloupe.

H. A. (overprint on stamps of Russia)—Siberia.

HAUTE - SENEGAL - NIGER—Upper Senegal
and Niger.

HAUTE SILESIA—Upper Silesia.

HAUTE VOLTA—Upper Volta.

H. B. A. (overprint on Russian stamps)—Siberia.

HELVETIA—Switzerland.

HERZOGTHUM HOLSTEIN, HERZOGTH.
SCHLESWIG—Schleswig-Holstein.

HIRLAPJEGY—Hungary.

HnEIPOE—Epirus.

HOBy—Montenegro.

HOI HAO (overprint on stamps of Indo-China)—
France.

HOLKAR—India, native state of Indore.

HRVATSKA—Croatia or Jugoslavia.

HYDERABAD—India, native state.

IDAR—India, native state.

I. E. F. (Indian Expeditionary Forces)—India.

IIAPA - IIAPE—Serbia or Montenegro.

IIETb—Bulgaria.

IIOIIITE—Montenegro.

IIOPTO MAPKA—Serbia.

IIOWTA IIAPA—Serbia.

IIOYIIIA - IIOYTA—Russia.

IIOYTA PYCCHON APMIN (overprint on Russian stamps)—Russia, Offices in Turkey.

IIPHA TOPA—Montenegro.

ILES WALLIS et FUTUNA—Wallis and Futuna Islands.

INDE—French India.

INDE FCAISE (overprint)—French India.

INDIA PORTUGUEZA—Portuguese India.

INDOCHINE—Indo-China.

INDONESIA (overprint on stamps of Dutch Indies)—Indonesia.

INDORE—India, native state.

INSTRUCCION—Venezuela.

IONIKON—Ionian Islands.

IQUIQUE (overprint on Chilean stamps)—Peru, under Chilean occupation.

IRANIENNES—Iran (Persia).

IRAQ (overprint on Turkish stamps)—Mesopotamia.

ISLAND—Iceland.

ISOLE ITALIAN DELL'EGEO (overprint on Italian stamps)—Italy - Aegean Islands.

ISOLE JONIE (overprint on Italian stamps)—Italian occupation of Ionian Islands.

ISTRIA—Jugoslavia.

ITA-KARJALA (overprint on stamps of Finland)—Karelia, under Finnish military administration.

ITALIA, ITALIANE—Italy.

JAFFA (overprint on stamps of Russia)—Russia, Offices in Turkey.

JAIPUR—India, native state.

JANINA (overprint on stamps of Italy)—Italy, Offices in Turkey.

JAVA (overprint)—Dutch Indies.

JEEND STATE—India (Jhind) native state.

JERUSALEM (overprint on stamps of Russia)—
Russia, Offices in Turkey.
JHALAWAR—India, native state.
JHIND - JIND—India, native state.
JOHORE—Straits Settlements.

KALAYAAN NAN PILIPINAS—Philippines,
Japanese occupation.
KAMERUN—Cameroons.
KAPUATCbKA-YKPAIHA (on Cesko-Slovensko
stamps)—Carpatho-Ukraine (Czechoslovakia).
KARJALA—Karelia.
KARKI (overprint on Italian stamps)—Italy,
Aegean Islands.
KARNTEN ABSTIMMUNG (overprint on
Austrian stamps)—Carinthia.

KAROLINEN—Caroline Islands.
KASHMIR—India, native state.
KATHIRI—Aden.
K. CPbCKA IIOIIITA—Serbia.
KEDAH—Straits Settlements.
KELANTAN—Straits Settlements.
KEMAHKOTAAN—Straits Settlements.
KERASSUNDE (overprint on stamps of Russia)
—Russia, Offices in Turkey.
KETAHKOTAAN—Straits Settlements.

K. G. C. A. (overprint on stamps of Jugoslavia)—
Carinthia.
K. G. L.—Danish West Indies or Denmark.
KGL. POST FRM—Denmark.
KH. CPN. IIOIITA—Serbia.
KIAUTSCHOU—Kiauchau.
KIONGA (overprint on stamps of Lourenco
Marques)—Kionga.
KISHANGARH—India, native state.
KLAIPEDA—Memel.

KONGELIGT—Danish West Indies or Denmark.
KORCA, KORCE—Albania.
KOUANG-TCHEOU (overprint on Indo-
Chinese stamps)—France, Offices in China.
KPAJbEBCTBO C. X. C.—Jugoslavia.
KPAJbEBNHA, KRALJEVINA, KRAL-
JEVSTVO—Jugoslavia.
KPHTH—Crete.
KRAIb. UPHATOPA—Montenegro.

KROON—Estonia.

K. U. K.—Austria or Bosnia and Herzegovina.

K. U. K. FELDPOST—Austria.

K. U. K. MILITARPOST—Bosnia and Herzegovina.

K. U. K. MILIT. - VERWALTUNG (overprint on military stamps of Austria)—Montenegro.

KUWAIT (overprint on Indian stamps)—Kuwait.

LA CANEA (overprint on Italian stamps)—Italy, Offices in Crete.

LAIBACH—Jugoslavia.

LAS BELA—India, native state.

LATTAQUIE (overprint on stamps of Syria)—Latakia.

LATVIJA, LATWIJA—Latvia.

LERO (overprint on Italian stamps)—Italy - Aegean Islands.

LEVANT (accompanied by words "Poste Francaise")—France, Offices in Turkey.

LEVANT (overprint on stamps of Great Britain)—Great Britain, Offices in Turkey.

LEVANT (overprint on stamps of Poland)—Poland, Offices in Turkey.

LIBAN, LIBANAISE—Lebanon.

LIBAU (overprint on stamps of Germany)—Latvia.

LIBYA (overprint)—United Kingdom of Libya.

LIETUVA, LIETVOS—Lithuania.

LIMA (overprint on stamps of Chile)—Peru, Chilean occupation.

L'ININI—Inini.

LIPSO (overprint on Italian stamps)—Italy - Aegean Islands.

LISSO (overprint on Italian stamps)—Italy - Aegean Islands.

LITWA LITWY—Central Lithuania.

LITWA SRODKOWA—Central Lithuania.

LJUBLJANSKA—Jugoslavia, under German occupation.

L. MARQUES (overprint on stamps of Mozambique)—Lourenco Marques.

L'OCEANIA—French Oceania.

L. P. (overprint on Russian stamps)—Latvia.

LUXEMBOURG—Luxemburg.

LUXEMBURG (overprint on German semi-postal stamps)—German occupation of Luxemburg.

MACAU, MACAV—Macao.
MAFEKING BESIEGED (overprint on Bechuanaland Protectorate and Cape of Good Hope stamps)—Cape of Good Hope.
MAGDALENA—Colombia.
MAGYAR, MAGYARORSZAG—Hungary.
MALAYA (without country name)—Straits Settlements.
MALMEDY (overprint on stamps of Belgium)—Belgian occupation of Germany.
MARIANAS ESPANOLAS (overprint on the stamps of the Philippines)—Marianna Islands.
MARIANEN—Marianna Islands.
MAROC—France, Offices in Morocco.

MAROCCO (overprint on stamps of Germany)—Germany, Offices in Morocco.
MARRUECOS—Spanish Morocco.
MARSHALL INSELN—Marshall Islands.
MAURITANIE—Mauritania.
MBLEDHJA KUSTETJESE—Albania, under Italian dominion.
MECKLBG VORPOMM—Germany (Russian Zone).
MECKLENB SCHWERIN—Mecklenburg Schwerin.
MECKLENB STRELITZ—Mecklenburg Strelitz.

M. E. F. (overprint on stamps of Great Britain)—Great Britain, Offices abroad.
MEJICO—Mexico.
MEMELGEBIET—Memel.
MENGE—Outer Mongolia.
METELIN (overprint on stamps of Russia)—Russia, Offices in Turkey.
MILIT POST PORTOMARKE—Bosnia and Herzegovina.
MILL or MILLIEMES (surcharge on stamps of France)—France, Offices in Egypt.

MN—Korea.
MOCAMBIQUE—Mozambique.
MODONES—Modena.

MONGTSEU (overprint on stamps of Indo-China)—France, Offices in China.

MONGTZE (overprint on stamps of Indo-China)—France, Offices in China.

MONT ATHOS (overprint on Russian stamps)—Russia, Offices in Turkey.

MONTSERRAT (overprint on stamps of Antiqua)—Montserrat.

MORA—Ukraine.

MOROCCO AGENCIES—Great Britain, Offices in Morocco.

MORVI—India, native state.

MOYEN CONGO—Middle Congo.

MQE (overprint on stamps of French Colonies)—Martinique.

M. V. I. R. (overprint)—Roumania, under German occupation.

NABHA—India, native state.

NACIONES UNIDAS—United Nations.

NANDGAM—India - Nandgaon, native state.

NAPOLETANA—Two Sicilies.

NA SLASK (overprint)—Central Lithuania.

NAURU (overprint on stamps of Great Britain)—Nauru.

N. C. E. (overprint on stamps of France)—New Caledonia.

NED. ANTILLEN—Netherlands Antilles (formerly Curacao).

NEDERLAND—Netherlands.

NED. INDIE, NEDERLANDSCH INDIE—Dutch Indies.

NEGRI SEMBILAN—Straits Settlements.

NEW HEBRIDES CONDOMINIUM (overprint on stamps of Fiji)—New Hebrides, British and French joint government.

NEZAVISNA—Croatia.

NIEUW GUINEA—Dutch New Guinea.

NISIRO (overprint on stamps of Italy)—Italy-Aegean Islands.

NIUE (overprint on stamps of New Zealand)—Niue.

NOPTOMAPKA—Montenegro.

NOPTO PORTO—Serbia.

NORDDEUTSCHER POSTBEZIRK—Germany, North German Postal District.

NORGE—Norway.
NOUVELLE CALEDONIE—New Caledonia.
NOUVELLE HEBRIDES—New Hebrides.
NOWANUGGUR—India, native state.
NOYT MAPKA—Azerbaijan.
NOYTA—Russia.
N. S. B. (overprint on stamps of France)—Nossi Be.
N. SEMBILAN—Straits Settlements.
N. S. W.—New South Wales.
NYASSA (overprint on stamps of Mozambique)—Nyassa.

OAHAMAPKA—Finland.
OAXACA—Mexico.
OCCUPATION FRANCAISE (overprint on stamps of Hungary)—French occupation of Hungary.
OCEANIE—French Oceania.
OESTERREICH, OFTERREICH, OSTER-REICH—Austria.
OFFENTLIG SAK—Norway.
OIL RIVERS—Niger Coast.
OKCA—Russia (Army of the North Issue).
OLTRE GIUBA (overprint on Italian stamps)—Italian Jubaland.
ORANJE VRIJ STAAT—Orange River Colony.
ORCHA—India, native state.
OR K. C. NOVITA—Serbia.
OSTERREICH (inscribed under post-horn)—Austria, Allied Military Government of Austria.
OSTLAND (overprint on stamps of Germany)—German occupation of Russia.
OTTOMANES—Turkey.
OUBANGUI - CHARI—Ubangi.

P. with star and crescent in circle (overprint on stamps of Straits Settlements)—Straits Settlements - Perak.
PACKHOI, PAK-HOI (on stamps of Indo-China)—France, Offices in China-Packhoi.
PAHANG—Straits Settlements.
PAKISTAN (overprint on stamps of India)—Pakistan.
PATIALA—India, native state.

PATMOS (overprint on stamps of Italy)—Italy - Aegean Islands.

P. C. C. P.—Russia.

P. D. and numeral (on stamps of French Colonies) —St. Pierre and Miquelon.

PECHINO (overprint on stamps of Italy)—Italy, Offices in China.

PENANG—Straits Settlements.

PERAK—Straits Settlements.

PERLIS—Straits Settlements.

PERSANE—Persia (Iran).

PERUANA—Peru.

PHILIPPINES (overprint on stamps of the United States)—Philippine Islands, under U.S. dominion.

P I (surcharged on stamps of Turkey)—Thrace.

PILIPINAS—Philippines, under Japanese occupation.

PINGIN—Ireland.

PISCOPI (overprint on stamps of Italy)—Italy - Aegean Islands.

PLEBISCITE OLZSTYN ALLENSTEIN (overprint on stamps of Germany)—Allenstein.

PLEBISCIT SLESVIG—Schleswig.

POCCIR—Russia or South Russia.

POCZTA LITWA SRODKOWA—Central Lithuania.

POCZTA POLSKA (overprint on stamps of Germany)—Poland; (overprint on stamps of Austria)—Germany, under Polish occupation.

P. O. II. N. T. (overprint on stamps of Russia)— Ukrainia.

POLSKA—Poland.

PORT GDANSK (overprint on stamps of Poland) —Poland, Offices in Danzig.

PORT-SAID—France, Offices in Egypt.

POSSEEL-POSTAGE—Union of South Africa.

POSTAGE - I.E.F.'D (overprint on stamps of Turkey)—Mesopotamia.

POSTAGE - POSTAGE & REVENUE (when on stamp with picture of King or Queen and denomination in penny, pence, pound or shilling) —Great Britain.

POSTAGE DUE (with denomination in pence or shilling)—Australia or Great Britain.

POSTEKHEOEUIEEGIZIANE—Egypt.

POSTE AERIEO - POSTE AERIENNE (on stamps without country name)—Persia.

POST SCHILLING (on stamps without country name)—Schleswig-Holstein.

POSTZEGEL (without mention of country name)—Netherlands.

PREUSSEN—Prussia.

PROTECTORATE FRANCAIS (overprint on stamps inscribed "Chiffre Taxe")—France, Offices in Morocco.

P. S. N. C. (ship in center - one letter in each corner of stamp)—Peru.

PTO. RICO, PUERTO RICO (overprint on United States stamps)—Puerto Rico, under U.S. dominion.

PUTTIALA—India, native state.

PYb, PYB—Finland, Russia or South Russia.

PYCCHON APMIN (overprint on stamps of Russia)—Russia, Offices in Turkey (Wrangel Issues).

PYCCKAR HOYTA (overprint on stamps of Russia)—Russia, Offices in Turkey (Wrangel Issues).

QARKU—Albania.

QATAR—A Sheikdom under British protection.

QINDAR, QINTAR—Albania.

QU'AITI—Aden.

R and numeral value (overprint on stamps of France and French Colonies)—Reunion.

R and numeral value plus additional overprint (overprint on stamps of France and French Colonies)—India - Jhind.

RAROTONGA—Cook Islands.

REGNO D'ITALIA—Italy; when overprinted with the words, "VENEZIA GIULIA" or with "TRENTINO"—Austria, under Italian occupation; when overprinted on stamps inscribed, "FIVME" or "FIUME"—Fiume.

REICHSPOST—Germany.

REIS (with no country name shown)—Portugal.

REP. DI S. MARINO—San Marino.

REPUB. FRANC, REPUBLIQUE FRANCAISE, R. F.—France or French Colonies, general issue.

REPUBLICA DOMINICANA—Dominican Republic.

REPUBLICA MOCAMBIQUE (overprint)—Mozambique.

REPUBLICA ORIENTAL—Uruguay.

REPUBLIK INDONESIA SERIKAT—United States of Indonesia.

RETYMNO—Crete.

RHEINLAND-PFALZ—Germany (French Occupation).

RIALAR SEALDAC NA HEIREANN (overprint on stamps of Great Britain)—Ireland.

RIZEH (overprint on stamps of Russia)—Russia, Offices in Turkey.

RL. PLATA F.—Cuba or Philippines.

R. O. (overprint on stamps of Turkey)—Eastern Roumelia.

RODI (overprint on stamps of Italy)—Italy - Aegean Islands.

ROMAGNE, ROMANA, ROMANIA—Roumania.

ROUMELIE ORIENTALE (overprint on stamps of Turkey)—Eastern Roumelia.

ROYAUME DE L'ARABIE SOUDITE ("Kingdom of Saudi Arabia")—Nejd.

R. S. M. (Rep. San Marino)—San Marino.

RUANDA (overprint on stamps of Congo)—German East Africa.

RUANDA - URUNDI—Belgian East Africa.

RUFFIFCH - POLEN (overprint on stamps of Germany)—Poland, under German occupation.

RUMANIEN (overprint on stamps of Germany) —Roumania, under German occupation.

RUSSISCH - POLAN (overprint on stamps of Germany)—Poland, under German occupation.

S. A. (overprint with three-armed cross on stamps of Latvia)—Latvia, under Russian occupation.

SAARE (overprint on stamps of Germany)—Saar.

SAARGEBIET—Saar.

SACHSEN—Germany (Russian Zone).

SAHARA ESPANOL—Spanish Western Sahara.

SAHARA OCCIDENTAL—Spanish Western Sahara.

SALONICCO (overprint on stamps of Italy)—Italy, Offices in Turkey.

SALONIQUE (overprint on stamps of Russia)—Russia, Offices in Turkey.

SANTANDER—Colombia.

SAORSTAT EIREANN (overprint on stamps of Great Britain)—Ireland.

SARKARI—India - Soruth, native state.

SAURASHTA—India - Soruth, native state.

SCARPANTO (overprint on stamps of Italy)—Italy - Aegean Islands.

SCHILLINGE (without country name)—Mecklenburg - Schwerin.

SEGNATASSE—Italy.

SEJM WILNIE—Central Lithuania.

SELANGOR—Straits Settlements.

SEN, SN—Japan.

SENEGAMBIE ET NIGER—Senegambia and Niger.

SERBIEN (overprint on stamps of Austria or Bosnia)—Serbia, under Austrian occupation; (overprint on stamps of Jugoslavia)—Serbia, under German occupation.

SHANGHAI (overprint on U.S. stamps)—United States, Offices in China.

SHQUIPENIA, SHQIPENIE, SHQIPERIA, SHQIPERISE, SHQIPNIJA, SHQYPTARE—Albania.

S. H. S.—Jugoslavia.

SIBERSKE—Siberia.

SIMI (overprint on stamps of Italy)—Italy - Aegean Islands.

SIRMOOR—India, native state.

SLESVIG—Schleswig-Holstein.

SLOVENSKO—Czechoslovakia and Slovakia.

SLOVENSKY STAT (overprint on stamps of Czechoslovakia)—Czechoslovakia and Slovakia.

S. MARINO—San Marino.

SMIRNE (overprint on stamps of Italy)—Italy, Offices in Turkey.

SMYRNE (overprint on stamps of Russia)—Russia, Offices in Turkey.

S. O. 1920 (overprint on stamps of Czechoslovakia or Poland)—Eastern Silesia.

SOCIETE DES NATIONS (League of Nations)
—Switzerland.

SOKOLSKI SLET—Jugoslavia.

SOMALIA—Italian Somaliland.

SONORA—Mexico.

SORUTH—India, native state.

SOUDAN (overprint on stamps of Egypt)—
Sudan.

SOUDAN FRANCAIS—French Sudan.

SOURASHTRA—India - Soruth, native state.

SOWJETISCHE BESATZUNGS ZONE (overprint for use in Russian Zone)—Germany.

S. P. M. (overprint on stamps of French Colonies)
—St. Pierre and Miquelon.

SRODKOWA LITWA—Central Lithuania.

STADT BERLIN—Germany (Russian occupation zone).

STAMPALIA (overprint on stamps of Italy)—
Italy - Aegean Islands.

STATI PARMENSI—Parma.

S. THOME E. PRINCIPE—St. Thomas and
Prince Islands.

STOTHHKH—Bulgaria.

STTRSTA - VUJA—Jugoslavia - Trieste.

STT-VUJA (overprint for use in Trieste)—
Jugoslavia.

SUIDAFRIKA—South Africa.

SUIDWES AFRIKA—South West Africa.

SULTANAT D'ANJOUAN—Anjouan.

SUNGEI UJONG—Straits Settlements.

SUOMI—Finland.

SVERIGE—Sweden.

S. W. A. (overprint on stamps of Union of South
Africa)—South West Africa.

SWAZIELAND—Swaziland.

SYRIE, SYRIENNE—Syria.

TANGER (overprint on stamps of France)—
France, Offices in Morocco; (overprint on
stamps of Spain)—Spain, Offices in Morocco.

TANGIER—Great Britain, Offices in Morocco.

TCHAD—Chad.

TCHONGKING (overprint on stamps of Indo-
China)—France, Offices in China.

TELEGRAFOS—Philippine Islands.

THURINGEN—Germany (Russian Zone).

TIEN TSIN (overprint on stamps of Italy)—Italy, Offices in China.

TIMBRE TAXE (with numeral and no country name)—French Colonies (General Issue).

TOGA—Tonga.

TO PAY—Great Britain.

TOSCANO—Tuscany.

TOUVA—Tannu Tuva.

TRAITE DE VERSAILLES (overprint on stamps of Germany)—Allenstein.

TRAVANCORE—India, native state.

TREBIZONDE (overprint on stamps of Russia)—Russia, Offices in Turkey.

TRENGGANU—Straits Settlements.

TRENTINO (overprint on stamps of Austria)—Austria.

TRIPOLI—Tripolitania.

TRIPOLI (preceded by, "XII CAMPIONARIA")—Libya.

TUNIS, TUNISIE—Tunisia.

TURK, TURKIYE—Turkey.

UAPCTBO—Bulgaria.

U. F.—French Indo-China.

U. G. (accompanied by numeral)—Uganda.

UKRAINE (overprint on stamps of Germany)—Russia, under German occupation.

ULTRAMAR (and year date)—Cuba or Puerto Rico.

ULTRAMAR (and denomination in avos, reis or both)—Macao or Guinea.

URUNDI (overprint on stamps of Congo)—German East Africa.

VALLEES D'ANDORRE—Andorra.

VALONA (overprint on stamps of Italy)—Italy, Offices in Turkey.

VATICANE—Vatican City.

VENEZ, VENEZOLANO—Venezuela.

VENEZIA GIULIA, VENEZIA TRIDENTINA (overprint on stamps of Austria and Italy)—Austria, under Italian occupation.

VETEKEVERRIA—Albania.

VIET NAM—Indo-China.

V. R. SPECIAL POST (overprint on stamps of Transvaal)—Cape of Good Hope (British occupation).

V. U. J. A. S. T. T. (on stamps of Jugoslavia)—Trieste.

WADHWAN—India, native state.

WENDEN, WENDENSCHE—Russia - Wenden (former province).

WN, WON, WUN—Korea.

WURTTEMBERG—Germany (French occupation).

XEIMAPPA (part of overprint on Greek stamps)—Epirus.

XEJEPA—Montenegro.

YCCP (overprint on stamps of Russia)—Ukraine.

YCTAB—Montenegro.

YEN, YN—Japan.

YKPAIHCbKA—Ukraine.

YKP.H.P. (overprint on stamps of Austria and Bosnia)—Western Ukraine.

YUNNAN FOU (overprint on stamps of Indo-China)—France, Offices in China.

Z. AFR. REPUBLIEK—(South African Republic) Transvaal.

ZANZIBAR (overprint on stamps of France)—France, Offices in Zanzibar.

Z. A. R. (overprint on Cape of Good Hope stamps)—Cape of Good Hope (issued in Vryeburg - Boer occupation).

ZELAYA—Nicaragua.

ZONA DEOCUPATIE ROMANA (overprint on stamps of Hungary)—Hungary, under Roumanian occupation.

ZONA OCCUPATA FIUMANO KUPA (overprint on stamps of Jugoslavia)—Jugoslavia, under Italian occupation.

ZONE FRANCAISE—Germany, under French occupation.

ZRACNA POSTA—Zone B - Trieste - Issued by Jugoslav Military Government.

ZUID AFRIKAANSCHE (South Africa Republic)—Transvaal.

ZUIDWEST AFRIKA—South West Africa.

AFGHANISTAN   ARMENIA

AUSTRIA

BATUM   BOSNIA and HERZEGOVINA

BURMA (Japanese Occupation)   BULGARIA

CHINA

EGYPT

ETHIOPIA (ABYSSINIA)

GEORGIA

GREAT BRITAIN

GREAT BRITAIN

62

GREECE

HEJAZ

INDIA (Native States)

IRAN (PERSIA)

IRELAND

ISRAEL

JAPAN

KOREA

**MALAYA-STRAITS SETTLEMENTS
(Japanese Occupation)**

MANCHUKUO

63

MONTENEGRO

NEPAL

PHILIPPINES
(Japanese Occupation)

RUSSIA

RYUKYU ISLANDS

SIAM (THAILAND)

SPAIN

SWITZERLAND

TURKEY

Putting stamps in your album

When all of your stamps are sorted out by country, the next step is to get them into your album. You can start with any country you like, although it is a good idea to begin with those from which you don't have so many stamps and work up to those where you have a great many. Open your album to the pages for the country you are going to mount and look through the pictures. This will give you an idea of the kinds of stamps the country has and the order in which they are to be arranged on the pages. Now, spread out the stamps you have from that country and note which ones obviously

These stamps show different designs; yet, they are obviously part of the same "set" and should go together in your album.

"go together." They may be exactly the same designs but with different values, or they may show pictures of the same person, or be distinctive because of unusual size or shape.

Get any duplicate stamps together at this point. When you find duplicates, be sure to put the stamp in finest condition in your album. It's best not to mount any stamps until you have checked for duplicates; otherwise, as soon as you have a stamp hinged in place,

Try to avoid torn and creased stamps, "perfins" (stamps with perforated initials), straight edge, badly off-center and heavily cancelled stamps.

a better copy may turn up. Tears, heavy cancellations, creases and folds, faded colors, missing perforation teeth, poor centering, all detract from the attractiveness of a stamp. Few of your stamps will be perfect in every respect, but when you have more than one to choose from, be sure to mount the best you have.

Use your tongs to pick up a stamp and move it along the rows of illustrations in your album until you find the picture that is exactly the same or close enough so that you know it is part of the same set.

Look at your stamps carefully as you sort them out! These three German stamps look very much alike at first glance. Can you spot the differences in the inscription and the background behind the figure?

The lower value stamps are usually the ones illustrated, so when you pick up a stamp to mount, start with the lowest value if it is one of a series. When you locate the right space for the stamp, attach a hinge and put it down squarely in its space. Put the stamp right on top of the illustration, if identical. If it is a different value of the same set, mount it in one of the spaces to the right of the illustration. The spaces to the right may have printed descriptions of the value or color of the stamp that should go there. If not, make your own arrangement in the extra spaces with the lowest value to the left, the highest value to the right.

After a little trial and error, you should find spaces for all the stamps from your first country. If you do have a few stamps left over, check the unfilled spaces again to make sure you haven't overlooked the right space. Then look at the stamps you have mounted to be sure the loose stamps don't duplicate any stamps already in place. If you still don't find a place, check your stamp again to be positive you have it with the proper country. If it is the right country, and there is really no space for it, then it is either a scarce issue or a high value that the editors of the album left out, or a new issue released after the pages of your album were designed and printed. Add a page if you have a loose-leaf album, or mount the extra stamps in the margins near the other stamps of the country. You run into this problem most frequently with small albums since the editors can only provide spaces for a small percentage of the world's stamps and must leave out many stamps that even beginning collectors easily acquire. With small albums you will often find that spaces have been provided for only the lower values of a set. If you find yourself with too many extra stamps for which there are no spaces you can be pretty certain the album you have is not adequate for your collection.

Building the collection

After identifying and mounting a few thousand different stamps, you will get a good idea of what kinds of issues each country has. Most of the pages in your album will contain at least a few stamps, and the majority of stamp-issuing countries will be represented. But what about the remaining spaces? Packets are still the least expensive way to build up a general world-wide collection.

There is no point, however, in buying another world-wide packet if you bought one to start with. Another packet of the same size will contain just about the same stamps you already have; a bigger packet will have some new stamps, but only the number by which the second packet exceeds the first. You will have to buy packets now of individual countries or groups of countries. When you buy a packet of just one country you must at the start buy the biggest packet you ever plan to get, because the bigger packets always duplicate the contents of the smaller ones.

Buying packets of all different stamps from individual countries is the least expensive way of filling out a world-wide collection.

Most dealers have packets of British, French and Portuguese colonial stamps. Sometimes you can get packets by areas, such as Asia or Latin America. These packets combine many inexpensive stamps so the unit cost per stamp is low. Don't buy one of these area packets if they include countries from which you might want to buy individual packets later.

Going through your album from A to Z with packets is possible if you would enjoy doing it that way. You may have found some countries more interesting than others as you worked your way through the first world-wide packet and you may prefer to build up your collection of those countries first. If this is so, you will probably want to get the bigger, more expensive packets of just these countries rather than smaller packets of many countries.

On the other hand, you may be anxious to increase the number of stamps in your album. The unit cost per stamp is much less for countries that have issued lots of stamps than for countries that have not used so many. Even though Great Britain was the first nation to use postage stamps, its issues have been conservative and a packet of 300 different at about $30 is the biggest most dealers have — cost per stamp is about 10c. On the other hand, Hungary has issued a great many stamps and a packet of 200 different Hungarian costs $1.50 or less — cost per stamp is about ¾c. You can buy as many as 1,000 different Hungarian stamps in a packet for about $20 — cost per stamp about 2c., still less than the unit cost of English stamps. Looking at it another way, $30 spent on English stamps will add 300 stamps to your collection but $10 spent on Hungarian stamps will add 600 stamps to your collection. If you are more interested in stamps of Great Britain than in the Hungarian issues you should buy the English stamps: they cost more and are worth more. However, if your interest is primarily in building up the number of stamps in your collection, the unit cost per stamp is an aspect that you should consider. Other countries whose stamps are available in large packets at small unit cost are Austria, Belgium, Czechoslovakia, France, Germany, Italy, Netherlands, Poland, Rumania, Russia, Spain and Turkey.

The country packets will have some duplicates of the stamps of each country you got in your world-wide packet. Save the duplicates as trading stock; be sure to compare the condition of the newly acquired stamp with the one already in your album. If the old one is not as good, replace it. Try to "upgrade" the condition of your stamps this way every chance you get.

After you have added the contents of an individual nation's packet to your album, you should have a good showing on that country's pages. If you want to fill the remaining spaces, you will have to purchase specific sets or singles from dealers' catalogues or stock books, or look through approval selections for the stamps you need, or trade duplicates with your stamp pals.

Recent issues are available from dealers in unused sets.

By the time you exhaust the possibilities for packet material, though, you will probably decide to confine your activities to building up some special country or group of countries or to a topic that appeals to you. After you have gone through the initial stage of general collecting and handled the stamps of many countries, you will probably want to concentrate on a project that holds promise of being completed within a reasonable length of time.

Older, scarcer stamps are sold as singles from dealer's stock books.

Most collectors sooner or later do decide to limit their serious collecting, although most of them maintain their world-wide collection to some extent.

69

5. Limiting Your Collection

The ideal of everyone who takes up stamp collecting as a hobby is to have every postage stamp ever issued and one each of all those still to come. You soon realize that any plan to get a copy of every stamp is doomed to frustration at the start. Many of the old stamps are scarce and therefore expensive; many are not even readily available at any price. Every day sees a new issue come out somewhere in the world and even the most industrious collector or dealer would be hard pressed to keep up with all of them.

The solution is to limit your serious collecting to some workable project. Nearly everyone looks forward to completing a project. The need to specialize if you want to complete anything becomes apparent as you advance through the introductory phase of general collecting. You can set a reachable goal for yourself by concentrating

One of the advantages of limiting your collection is that you have time to learn the story behind each of your stamps. These two Danish stamps refer to the Hans Christian Andersen fairy tales, "The Ugly Duckling" and "The Little Mermaid."

on stamps of one country or a group of countries, or on one kind of stamp, such as airpost issues or topical stamps that are related to one another by pictorial design, such as animals on stamps.

U.S. issues make a fine specialized collection; they cover almost the whole period of time that adhesive postage stamps have been in use. There are rarities, but every issue has some common stamps and can at least be represented at modest cost; the commemoratives cover a wide range of important subjects; and there are many new issues every year to sustain your interest. The stamps of Canada and Mexico and the other American republics are also popular countries for specialization. European stamps arouse the interest of many

Canadian and Mexican stamps are very popular with American collectors.

collectors because of our common heritage. On the other hand, your taste may run toward the lesser known countries of Asia or

Independence issue of Ghana, one of several newly independent nations whose complete stamp issues are still available.

Africa. Newly independent nations have a special appeal—you can easily begin with their first stamps and maintain a complete collection.

These maps show the extent of the British and French colonial empires.

By specializing in colonial issues, you can have a world-wide but still limited collection. British and French colonial issues especially are extensive, but there are also stamps of Portuguese, German and Belgian colonies and others. The "Benelux" countries, Belgium, Netherlands and Luxembourg, are often grouped together as a specialized collection. Other popular groups are British North America, the West Indies, Scandinavia, Oceania and Central Europe.

Both Scott and Minkus Publications have a line of specialty albums for the popular countries.

You will be glad to find that special albums are available for individual countries and for some groupings. The specialized albums have a space for every stamp issued by the country. Rarities, varieties and high values are not left out as they are in world-wide albums. Every space has an illustration or a description of the stamp intended for it. The pages present a perfect guide for you to follow in developing your collection. To give you some suggestions for possibilities in limiting your collection, the following list shows the specialized albums available from various manufacturers:

Afghanistan, Iran-Persia
Africa, Independent Countries
Asia, Independent Countries
Austria
Belgium & Colonies
Brazil
British Africa
British America
British Asia
British Europe
British Oceania
Canada
Cambodia, Laos, Vietnam
Central Europe
Chile, Peru
Colombia, Panama & Canal Zone
Czechoslovakia
Ecuador, Venezuela
France
French Africa
Germany
Ghana

Greece
India
Ireland
Israel
Italian Colonies
Italy
Japan
Latin West Indies
Liechtenstein
Luxemburg
Mexico
Monaco, Andorra
Netherlands & Colonies
Portugal & Colonies
Scandinavia & Baltic Countries
South America
Soviet Republics
Spain & Colonies
Switzerland
Tunisia, Libya & Morocco
United Nations
Vatican City

Begin your specialized collection by transferring the stamps for the chosen country from your world-wide general album to your new specialty album. With a general collection, you concentrate on the stamps you have; with a specialized collection, you will be more and more aware of empty spaces, the missing stamps. You will see where you have incomplete sets, where you have both used and unused stamps, and when your stamps are singled out, you will note that some are not in very good condition. Your first concern as a specialist collector will be filling in the empty spaces. Improving the appearance of your collection by upgrading the condition of your stamps will be the second. If the issues of the country you have chosen are at all extensive, you will find you have blank spaces not

Specialist collectors are interested in varieties as well as face-different stamps. Here are three French stamps with slight variations in their designs. (Left) Horizon line with sun at right, (center) solid background, feet on base, (right) solid background, no base under feet.

only for "face different" stamps but for "varieties" as well. Perforation and watermark varieties occur in the issues of many countries. Nearly all stamps have perforations and a good many are printed on watermarked paper. These two factors become important when you have to differentiate between otherwise identical stamps. Two stamps can be exactly alike except for a difference in their perforation measurement or the watermark in the paper on which they are printed.

Perforations

The number of holes within a space of 20 millimeters (this is about ¾ of an inch) along the side of a stamp is the "gauge" of the perforations. Determining the gauge is easy: just run the edge of a stamp along the face of a metal gauge finder (called a perforation gauge) until the perforations match one of the rows of dots. Stamps

Perforation gauge

are described as "perf 10, perf $10\frac{1}{2}$," etc. The horizontal (top and bottom) gauge is customarily given first if it is different from the gauge of the vertical edges (sides), for example, "perf $11 \times 10\frac{1}{2}$". Much experimenting with perforation was done in earlier years and you are more likely to find perforation varieties on older stamps. Most countries now have a standard perforation which they use on

These four stamps show the same design but are differently perforated. (1) perf 12, (2) compound perforation, perf 11 x 10, (3) coil stamp, horizontal perf 8 ½, (4) coil stamp, vertical perf 10.

all issues. "Coil stamps" are a special type produced in roll form for stamp-vending machines. They are perforated on two edges only, either the two horizontal or the two vertical edges.

Watermarks

Watermarks, too, create varieties. Stamps that are identical in design may have been printed on sheets of paper with different watermarks or sometimes on watermarked and unwatermarked paper. Designs or lettering are impressed in the paper during its manufacture. The paper is thinner where the design has been impressed and it shows up when the paper is held in front of a light. The outline that you see is called a watermark. Once the paper has

74

been printed on, it is not so easy to see the watermark clearly. You can use a watermark tray, a shallow black dish, to bring it out again. Dealers sell the trays for about $1.00. Place your stamp face down in the tray and pour in a little benzene or one of the trade name detector fluids. Carbon tetrachloride will work as a detector fluid, but using it can be dangerous since its fumes are harmful when inhaled. As the paper absorbs the fluid, the thin part (the watermark) appears dark in contrast to the rest of the paper. Waving the stamp in the air with your tongs will dry it in just a few seconds.

With a watermark tray and fluid you can detect the watermarks in the paper on which stamps are printed. The stamp in the upper right corner of the tray is the German stamp above. When it is put in the tray and covered with fluid its watermark shows up like the drawing at the right.

Popular watermarks are small devices, such as crowns, crosses, flowers and monograms, and at least one complete design shows up on each stamp. A few stamps are printed on sheets of paper with an overall watermark—wavy lines or lozenges which are still clear enough on individual stamps. Other watermarks, such as coats of arms or a series of letters, spread over a whole sheet, but only a small portion shows on any one stamp. Your album or catalogue will tell you what to look for.

Stamp conditions

When you first start collecting, condition is always secondary to filling another space. As you develop into a sophisticated, discerning collector, condition will become much more important. When you begin buying stamps that cost a few dollars each, condition will be a determining factor in every purchase.

Stamps in choice condition are certainly more pleasing to own and display. The finer they are, the more desirable and hence more valuable they are likely to become. Whenever possible, you should get stamps in the best condition available; just as you learn to compare duplicates in your world-wide collection, now you must learn to choose from among the stamps offered for sale. Until you are sure of what you are doing, however, don't pay heavy premiums for superior condition stamps. Remember you can still enjoy a less-than-perfect stamp; its historical appeal at least is just the same as that of a better copy. Condition is something you should know about, but not become obsessed with—if you pay a premium for a stamp in superior condition, you want to be sure you are getting what you pay for; if you are offered a terrific bargain, you should know that poor condition may well be the reason for it.

Collectors use the following terms to describe the condition or state of preservation of stamps. By studying these terms you will know what to expect when you buy stamps; by applying your own stamps to these standards you can judge the condition of your own collection:

SUPERB—A stamp described as superb must be perfect in every respect. The color must be bright, clean and unsoiled. The centering must be perfect, with even margins all around. No perforation teeth may be missing. Imperforate stamps must have ample margins on all sides. The slightest thin spot, a crease or a tear would disqualify a stamp. Mint stamps must have their full original gum (o.g.). Used stamps must be clearly, lightly and neatly cancelled. Many issues, particularly older stamps, are virtually unobtainable in superb condition.

VERY FINE—Very fine stamps are well above average and highly desirable. The color must not be faded and such a stamp must be unsoiled. It will be well centered, with ample margins all around, although not necessarily perfectly even. The perforations must be intact and the stamp free of any defects in the paper. Mint stamps have full original gum; used stamps have reasonably light cancellations.

FINE—The term, fine, describes an attractive stamp that is not quite as bright or as well centered as a Very Fine copy. The margins are usually uneven, but the perforations should not cut into the frame line of the printed design at any point. It may have a few short perforations, but none should be missing completely. The paper should be free of defects. A mint stamp must have gum, but it may show some heavy hinge marks. Used stamps may be heavily cancelled, but not so heavily that important parts of the design are obliterated.

GOOD—The average stamp found in packets, mixtures and approval books falls into this category. Good stamps are often far off center, heavily cancelled but not obliterated, even lightly creased. They must not, however, have tears or bad thin spots.

POOR—Not much is expected of stamps in this category. Poor stamps may be heavily cancelled and perforations may cut far into the design. Some perforations may be missing; the stamp may be slightly torn or heavily creased.

BAD and DAMAGED describe stamps that are highly undesirable. They usually have tears or other extreme faults and are best left out of your album.

Filling out your collection

By limiting your collection, you can afford to look into some of the philatelic speciality items that add impressive touches to a display of stamps.

STAMPS ON COVER—A whole envelope, a cover, shows more of the postal markings than can appear on single stamps. The postmark shows the city and date where and when the cover was mailed. Many countries use special commemorative slogans. If you are specializing in the stamps of one area, you will certainly want to keep up with current events as reflected on their mail.

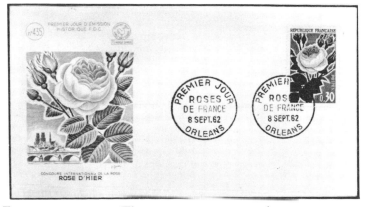

FIRST-DAY COVERS—These are covers carrying a new stamp cancelled on its first day of use with an appropriate inscription. This is a different way of adding the new issues of your chosen country to your collection. Many first-day covers have attractive printed cachets (legends) pertaining to the purpose of the issue.

MAXIMUM CARDS— Collectors use stamps on the picture side of post-cards with designs similar or related to the design of the stamp as an outstanding way to complement and call attention to the beautiful designs of the stamps.

79

COMMÉMORANT LE QUINZIÈME ANNIVERSAIRE
COMMEMORATING THE FIFTEENTH ANNIVERSARY

UNITED NATIONS DAY, 24 OCTOBER 1960 · JOURNÉE DES NATIONS UNIES, 24 OCTOBRE 1960

SOUVENIR SHEETS—With stamp collectors in mind, many postal departments, including the U.S., issue small sheets. The margins of most of these sheets contain printed legends relating to the event or purpose for which the sheet was issued.

Unused blocks of stamps make an attractive showing on an album page. It is also a way to hold extra stamps as an investment.

BLOCKS OF STAMPS—If one stamp looks good, wouldn't four stamps be four times as attractive? Some collectors mount unsevered blocks, usually four stamps, in their album. This is common practice among those who buy for investment. Investors buy every new issue in blocks of four in the hope that they can some day sell three of the stamps for the price they paid for the block of four. In the meantime, a block of stamps makes quite a showing in their album.

The number is that of the plate from which the stamps were printed. It appears on each pane of 50, 70 or 100 stamps and four panes with the same number are printed from each plate. The number can appear in four different positions, lower right (shown), lower left, upper left and upper right. A plate block of the same number from each of the four positions is a "matched set."

PLATE-NUMBER BLOCKS—This term especially applies to U.S. and Canadian stamps. It refers to a block that has the part of the margin that shows the number of the printing plate from which the stamps were printed. Plate-number blocks are scarcer than regular blocks or single stamps since the number appears only once on each pane (usually 50, 70, or 100 stamps).

There are many inducements for limiting your collection—the likelihood of completing a project, the chance to study each stamp in detail, and the many special items that add glamor to a collection. With so many possibilities for specialized collecting, you may have trouble making a choice. One of the main reasons for starting with the general collection was to acquaint yourself with stamps of many countries, so you could discover what interests you the most.

U.S. issues will surely catch your attention before you have been collecting for very long, if indeed they weren't the reason you took up collecting in the first place. Attractive new commemoratives are in the news every few months and this alone is responsible for nearly every American collector's maintaining an interest in U.S. stamps in addition to whatever else he is working on.

6. United States Stamps

Following Great Britain's lead, the United States was one of the first nations to use adhesive postage stamps. Like the Penny Black, the early U.S. issues were printed on imperforate sheets and the individual stamps had to be cut apart with scissors. On the so-called "stampless covers" that had gone before, the postmaster had to write or mark in ink the amount of postage paid and the name of the city from which the letter was being sent. And the writer could take his letter to the post office and prepay the fee only during its business hours; there was no such thing as a corner mail box.

The first United States stamps were these 5¢ and 10¢ values issued in 1847.

The first U.S. stamps

Distribution of the first government-issued postage stamps took place during July of 1847. The first issue was just two denominations, a 5c. red-brown stamp for ordinary letters going less than 300 miles and a 10c. black stamp for letters going farther. A portrait of Benjamin Franklin appears on the 5c. value and George Washington is shown on the 10c. stamp. The Continental Congress chose Franklin as the first postmaster general in 1775 and he was given the place of honor on the first stamp as the "father" of the American postal system. The first president, George Washington, was as much revered at that time as he is today. These two men have appeared on more U.S. stamps than any other person.

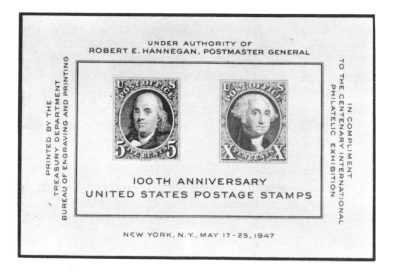

Although large numbers of both stamps were issued during the four years they were in use, so many collectors want them for their albums that they are now fairly expensive. Choice copies of the 5c. 1847 cost about $750; the 10c. stamp sells for $1,750 or more. Fortunately, they are both reproduced on a 100th anniversary souvenir sheet issued by the post office in 1947 (see above for illustration). The reproductions are so faithful to the actual designs that the post office had to print them in different colors to prevent their being cut out of the sheet and sold as originals to uninformed collectors. This souvenir sheet with both stamps is available from dealers for less than a dollar. An interesting sidelight is that more than ten million sheets were sold in a few days as collectors' items, more than twice the number of originals that were sold during the four years from 1847 to 1851 when they were used for postage. Another unusual twist is that the replicas are valid for postage, but the originals were demonetized in 1851. The originals were prepared by a private firm of bank-note printers and their contract with the government allowed them to keep the plates from which the stamps were printed after the contract had expired! There was no reason to suspect they would go on printing stamps, but as a security measure the post office declared all stamps of that design invalid.

Early U.S. issues

Age is not a significant factor in determining the value of stamps. Some early adhesives were used in such large quantities that you can get them today for nominal prices. Many of the 19th century issues are rare and relatively expensive, but if you are concentrating on U.S. stamps you can at least represent each issue at little cost.

By 1851 the growing postal system needed more denominations of stamps to cover its services. The letter rate was reduced to 3c. for distances up to 3,000 miles. This rate applied to nearly all mail except letters sent coast to coast which had to go around Cape Horn in those days. A completely new set of stamps, 1c., 3c., 5c., 10c., and 12c., was prepared. So many millions of letters were carried under the new rate that you can buy the first 3c. stamp, now a hundred and twenty-five years old, for your collection at a cost of less than $2. Thomas Jefferson appeared for the first time on the new 5c. stamp.

(Left) Imperforate stamps of the 1851 issue. Imperforate pairs are much more desirable than single stamps and often cost several times as much. (Center) Beginning in 1857, stamps were issued with perforations for easier separation. (Right) Modified designs were used on the 1861 issue.

The old scissors work was done away with by 1857 when sheets were sent to the post offices with perforations punched between the stamps for easy separation. The stamps were printed so close together on the sheets though, that the perforations cut into the design of nearly every stamp. This is upsetting to collectors who insist on perfect copies of stamps this old; they are hard to find and bring high premiums when they do turn up.

At the outbreak of the Civil War, supplies of stamps in Southern post offices fell into the hands of the Confederacy. To prevent their being sent north and sold to furnish money for the South, all outstanding stamps were declared invalid for postage by the North and replaced by a series of altered designs. The portraits were about the same on the new stamps, but the framework was quite different.

On the new 2c. denomination, added to the series in 1863, is a portrait of Andrew Jackson that nearly covers the whole stamp. This unusual stamp, known as the "Black Jack," has always been popular with collectors. Another new value, printed in black, was a 15c. stamp issued just a year after Lincoln's assassination, mourning for the martyred President.

The pictorial issue of 1869. (Left) Pony Express rider, (center) early steam locomotive, (right) the steamship "Adriatic." Note the "bull's-eye" cancellation on the stamp at the left. The heavy cancellation on the stamp at the right is also typical of this period when hand-made cork cancellers were being used.

A whole new concept of stamp design was introduced by the issue of 1869. The stamps were square-shaped and pictorial views replaced the portraits on most values. These scenes of the Pony Express, an early steam locomotive, the steamship *Adriatic*, etc., which seem so attractive to us now, were unpopular at the time and the issue was discontinued in just a year.

Bank-note issues

Production of paper money was taken over by the Bureau of Engraving and Printing in Washington during the Civil War but the Post Office Department continued to award contracts to private firms for printing postage stamps. Replacing the then unpopular

pictorials came a new series of large-size portrait stamps again featuring busts of distinguished deceased Americans. Three companies held the contract during the years between 1870 and 1890 and American stamp specialists can identify the issues of each company by differences in the paper they used and minute changes, called "secret marks," in the design.

A more convenient small-size stamp was introduced in 1890. Enough mail was sent during these years for the stamps to be plentiful and you can represent many of the bank-note company issues through the 10c. value for less than $1 each. A penny reduction in the cost of sending a letter went into effect during 1883 and, since more of the basic rate stamps are used than any other denomination, you can put examples of the 2c. and 3c. bank-note issues in your collection for very little.

Fancy cancellations

Something to watch for on 19th century U.S. stamps are "fancy" cancellations. Besides the postmarks with the name of the city or the usual unexciting black splotch, you can sometimes find circles,

A star cancellation on an 1873 bank-note stamp. Fancy cancellations add to the value of a stamp and really unusual designs like a skull and crossbones can make a stamp worth several times the value of an ordinary copy.

crossroads, stars, etc. and if you are really lucky even find a kicking mule or a skull and crossbones. An unusual cancellation makes a stamp more interesting and always more valuable. Cancellation collectors have already picked over most of the stamps in dealers' stocks, but new material is always being turned up and "fancy cancels" are worth watching for.

Commemorative stamps

Chicago was the site of the World's Columbian Exposition celebrating the 400th anniversary of Columbus' discovery of America. Over 27 million admissions were recorded during the fair's six-month run in 1893. The number of admissions was equal to one-third of the total population of the United States, proof that this was considered one of the greatest events of all time. Stamp collectors were already numerous then and plans for publicizing the celebration included issuing a series of stamps depicting scenes of the life of Columbus. All together, 16 denominations from 1c. to $5 were released. The dollar values $1, $2, $3, $4, and $5, were higher than any ever issued before.

This wonderful set is in the dreams of every stamp collector and the degree of completeness of the "Columbians" is one standard by which advanced collections of U.S. stamps are judged. An unused set of all 16 values sells for more than $12,000 — quite an increase over the years from the original face cost of $16.34! Fewer than 25,000 copies were sold of the $3, $4, and $5 values, explaining their

The Columbian Exposition issue of 1893 features reproductions of paintings pertaining to Columbus' discovery of America. Each artist had his own ideas about Columbus' appearance, and this gave rise to an interesting "stamp story." The 1¢ value shows a clean-shaven Columbus in sight of land. The 2¢ value shows the landing of Columbus with a full-grown beard the very next day! This wins the award as the fastest-growing beard in history.

rarity on today's market when a few thousand stamps have to be divided among millions of collectors. Happily, the lower values are within the reach of every one. Nearly a billion and a half of the 2c. denomination were sold so you can get a used copy today for just a nickel.

The first set of U.S. commemorative stamps contained values ranging from 1¢ to $5.

The Columbians were available in post offices in addition to the then current, small-size bank-note stamps. They were not intended to replace the regular series and after a time, the unsold stamps were recalled and destroyed. This new idea, stamps prepared in limited quantities with designs suitable for release on special occasions, led to the long and still-continuing series of wonderful U.S. commemoratives. Significant events are recorded on U.S. stamps; great men are honored; and important historic occasions are recalled on the occasion of their anniversaries.

Following the Columbians, the next commemoratives were on a similar pattern, that is, a series of denominations with different designs related to a single theme. Collectors complained, however, about the expense of the high denominations and they were dropped. Expositions were a popular theme; series soon appeared for the 1898 Trans-Mississippi Exposition in Omaha, the 1901 Pan-American

The stamps of the 1898 Trans-Mississippi issue, a set of nine values from 1¢ to $2, carry scenes pertaining to the settlement of the Middle West.

The attractive $1 value of the 1898 Trans-Mississippi issue reproduces a painting by J. MacWhirter entitled "Western Cattle in a Storm."

at Buffalo, the 1904 St. Louis World's Fair, and the 1907 Jamestown Exposition at Hampton Roads, Virginia.

One of the purposes of the 1901 Pan-American Exposition was to pay tribute to the progress made in the fields of transportation and communication.

Three values of the Pan-American series turned up with inverted centers—the 1¢, 2¢ and 4¢. The stamps were printed in two colors which required each sheet to pass through the press twice. A few

The earliest inverted center errors on U.S. postage stamps occurred on the 15¢, 24¢ and 30¢ values of the 1869 pictorial series.

This stamp enlarged.

90

sheets apparently went wrong end first for the second color, producing these famous errors. There are thought to be 1,000 specimens of the 1c. inverts in existence, 160 of the 2c. value and about 200 of the 4c. denomination.

About 160 copies of this 2¢ red and black stamp of 1901 are known to exist with the center design printed upside down.

Similar errors have been discovered on the 15c., 25c. and 30c. values of the 1869 series of regular issue stamps. The most famous error, however, is the 24c. airmail stamp of 1918 with the airplane flying upside down. A single sheet of 100 stamps was inadvertently sold across a post office counter to a collector who immediately recognized the value of his find. A single stamp from this sheet now can bring more than $100,000!

Later commemorative issues, such as this set of three issued for the 1907 Jamestown Tercentenary Exposition, did not include high value stamps and so were more widely distributed on mail.

The 100th anniversary of Abraham Lincoln's birth in 1909 further refined the format for commemoratives. Only one denomination, the 2c. first-class letter rate, was issued, thus ensuring the

widest possible circulation during the time the stamp was used. Commemorative issues became more frequent — so much so that 1922 was the last year in which no issue was released. Averaging about two a month in recent years, the total number of U.S. commemoratives is now several hundred different stamps. A few sets have been issued recently, but the majority today are single stamps for the first-class letter rate currently in effect in the year of issue — 2c. until 1932, back up to 3c., raised to 4c. in 1957 and increased again to 5c., 6c., 8c., 10c., 13c., 15c., 18c., 20c., and now 22c.

These commemorative stamps create an interest in history and develop an awareness of the important people, events and themes of our national heritage—Columbus' discovery, the landing of the Pilgrims, the Declaration of Independence, the California Gold Rush, the battles of the Civil War, the invasion of Iwo Jima and many many others.

Among the sets of commemorative stamps, the 1934 National Parks issue, the Famous Americans series of 1940 and the Overrun Countries issue of 1943-44 have long been favorites. More recent sets include the American Credo series, the Historical Flags issue, and the continuing American Bicentennial releases.

The job of printing the 1943-44 Overrun Countries' Flags series was given out to the American Bank Note Co. of New York City in order to take advantage of their special multicolor printing equipment.

Subjects ranging from the poultry industry to a communications satellite, from newspaper boys to freedom of the press have been featured on U.S. commemorative stamps. Famous Americans from Alexander Hamilton to the late John Foster Dulles have been honored on recent postal issues. Leaders of other nations appear on the Champions of Liberty series started in 1957. The 8c. foreign surface-mail value has been used so that every part of the world can see the U.S. respects those who fight for freedom everywhere. Most issues also included a 4¢ value, then the domestic letter rate.

A series of stamps honoring the world's "champions of liberty" was released between 1957 and 1961.

New presses at the Bureau of Engraving and Printing can produce multi-colored stamps, outstanding examples of which are the Fine Arts series reproducing the work of famous artists including Frederic Remington and Winslow Homer.

Stamps in the Fine Arts series are reproduced in color: (right) "The Smoke Signal" by Frederic Remington and (left) "Breezing Up" by Winslow Homer.

The first of the annual U.S. Christmas stamps was released in 1962. Some of the more recent issues have featured full-color reproductions of works of religious art. Placed on sale from early November and available until the end of the year, these special stamps now have press runs of well over a billion copies each. For the Christmas issue of 1964 four different stamps were printed on the same sheet—a first in U.S. philatelic history.

Fittingly enough, the 1964 Christmas stamps were first put on sale at Bethlehem, Pennsylvania.

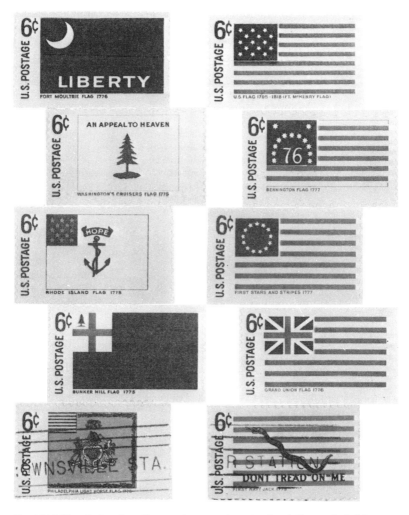

The 1968 Historic American Flags series reproduces ten Revolutionary Period banners in full color.

Another philatelic first occurred in 1968 when the Post Office produced the Historic American Flags set of ten stamps on a single pane of 50. The ten varieties were printed in vertical rows so that the same stamp appears horizontally in rows of five.

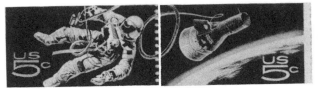

Still one more unusual stamp issue, a set of "twin" stamps, was created to salute America's accomplishments in space. The left stamp shows an astronaut walking in space; the right stamp pictures the Gemini IV spacecraft above the curve of the earth. The twin stamps, which can be divided along a central perforation, honor America's space program in general but refer specifically to the Gemini IV flight of June 3-7, 1965 in which Major Edward H. White became the first American to walk in space.

In the Beautification of America issue, four different stamp designs appear in the same sheet.

The Beautification of America issue of 1969 marked the second time that four different stamps were printed on the same sheet, and the first time that four designs appeared on a single pane of 50. Later in 1969, the XI International Botanical Congress issue, also consisting of four designs printed on a single pane of 50, made its appearance. These stamps all received immediate and wide acceptance for their attractiveness.

U.S. 6ᶜ POSTAGE

DWIGHT D. EISENHOWER

These jumbo stamps of 1969 honor the late President Dwight Eisenhower and American artist William M. Harnett.

SIX CENTS

UNITED STATES POSTAGE

AMERICAN PAINTING

WILLIAM M. HARNETT

Continuing its imaginative stamp program, the Post Office Department released three "jumbo" stamps in 1969. These are the largest U.S. postage stamps ever produced, measuring $1\frac{1}{4}$ by 2 inches. The first of these commemorated the moon landing on July 20, 1969. Even more exciting than the new large size of the stamp is the fact that the plates from which it was printed were made from a master steel die that had been carried aboard the Apollo II spacecraft itself on the round-trip journey to the moon.

This jumbo-sized 10¢ airmail stamp picturing an astronaut stepping onto the surface of the moon marks the lunar landing on July 20, 1969.

10¢ AIR MAIL

UNITED STATES

FIRST MAN ON THE MOON

After the moon landing commemorative was issued, the Post Office Department was deluged with so many first-day cancellation requests that it took nearly five months to complete the job. A record

8,743,070 first-day cancellations were applied to covers bearing the jumbo 10c. airmail stamp. This was nearly three times greater than the previous first-day cover record of approximately 3 million for the 4c. Project Mercury stamp issued in February, 1962..

The designs of the 1970 Natural History series stamps were based on exhibits which can be seen in the American Museum of Natural History in New York and a mural at the Peabody Museum at Yale University.

The next philatelic milestone was reached in 1970 with the set of four Natural History stamps issued to mark the 100th anniversary of the founding of the American Museum of Natural History in New York City. This jumbo size set was issued with the four different designs in a block.

Among the many individual commemoratives released in 1970 is this Stone Monument Memorial issue showing the granite carving that has become one of the wonders of the world.

The U.S. Postal Service continues to issue individual commemorative stamps of varying sizes, but because of the popularity of the Natural History issue, it emphasizes sets of regular and jumbo sizes in blocks ranging from two to ten stamps.

On July 1, 1971 the United States Postal Department became the United States Postal Service, a semi-independent organization. On this date a new 8c. stamp with the Postal Service emblem was issued simultaneously at all 33,000 post offices nationwide.

This twin stamp of 1971 marked a decade of extraordinary American accomplishment in the exploration of space. The right stamp shows the astronauts in a lunar rover; the left stamp shows the lunar lander on the moon's surface.

On August 2, 1971 the second twin stamp commemorating a Decade of Space Achievement was issued. As in the issue of 1967, each stamp is complete by itself, but together they make one design depicting Earth orbiting the moon on which a landing craft is seen in the background with the Astronauts in their Lunar Rover in the foreground. The first day of issue was celebrated at Kennedy Space Center, Florida; Houston, Texas; and the George C. Marshall Space Flight Center in Huntsville, Alabama.

Astronauts David R. Scott and James B. Irwin established the first post office on the moon when they cancelled the first letter there. The cancellation reads, "United States on the Moon, August 2, 1971." The envelope, a stamp pad, and a rubber postmarking device were in a container made of beta cloth, a material which can withstand a temperature of 2400°, attached under the driver's seat of the Lunar Rover.

99

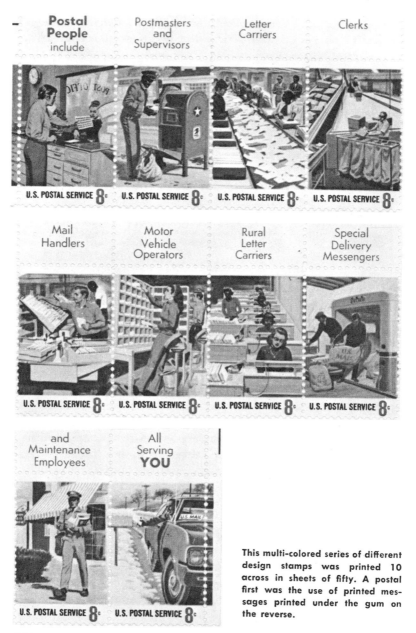

This multi-colored series of different design stamps was printed 10 across in sheets of fifty. A postal first was the use of printed messages printed under the gum on the reverse.

The Cape Hatteras Commemorative composed of four separate stamps forms a single square design.

The Cape Hatteras Commemorative issue of 1972 in the National Parks Centennial series, was the first U.S. block of four 2c. stamps to form a single square design, although each stamp in the set is complete in itself. Other stamps in the issue are Wolf Trap Farm, Virginia; Old Faithful, Yellowstone; and Mt. McKinley, Alaska.

The Postal Service Employees issue of April 30, 1973 introduced another innovation. Honoring the postal workers, it consists of 10 individual subjects printed in horizontal rows of ten in panes of 50. For the first time in postal history, each stamp bears a descriptive message printed under the adhesive on the reverse.

A new design treatment was employed for the set of four stamps commemorating America's Mineral Heritage issued June 13, 1974 at the National Gem and Mineral Show in Lincoln, Nebraska. Among the most handsome ever issued, the 8-color stamps are square, 1.075 by 1.075 inches each, and designed so that when rotated 45 degrees, individually or as a block, they form a nearly diamond shape. The denomination is horizontal only when the stamp is so rotated.

On November 15, 1974 the Christmas Stamp depicting the Dove of Peace Weathervane atop Mount Vernon was the first *self-adhesive* stamp ever to be issued. Released only as a precancelled stamp to test such precancellation to speed up seasonal mail, it was sold only through the post offices in the test areas—Allegheny, Chicago, Salt Lake City and Tampa.

As Christmas 1975 approached, it had not been decided whether a postal rate increase would go into effect before or after the holiday

The 1974 Mineral Heritage issue displays four different designs in sheets of 48 stamps.

season, and so the annual commemorative issue was printed without a denomination, for the first time in postal history. In 1978, also in anticipation of a rate increase, a regular-issue stamp bearing the letter "A" was issued (15c.), followed by "B" in 1981 (18c.), "C" later in 1981 (20c.), and "D" in 1985 (22c.).

U.S. Bicentennial Series

On July 4, 1971 the U.S. Postal Service inaugurated its series of stamps commemorating the Bicentennial of the American Revolution with the release of a stamp depicting the emblem of the Bicentennial Commission. Each year since then it has issued stamps either singly or in blocks of four with the Bicentennial emblem and inscription either on the stamp or in the block margin.

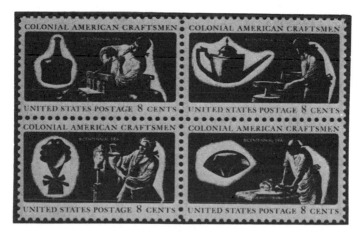

Several issues of stamps were released in conjunction with the Bicentennial celebrations to honor the people, places and events that led to the creation of the United States. This set of four pays tribute to colonial craftsmen—glassmaker, silversmith, wigmaker and hatter.

The set of 4 subjects issued on March 18, 1972 honors Colonial American Craftsmen. Four stamps, depicting communications in Colonial times, were issued individually between February and September 1973.

The block of four stamps commemorating the Boston Tea Party, issued on July 4, 1973, is a notable example of four self-contained stamps making a single design as a set. It depicts the scene in Boston Harbor in 1773 when colonists, protesting objectionable taxes, dumped chests of tea into the harbor.

The First Continental Congress of 1774 is commemorated in the block of four stamps issued on July 4, 1974. In March 1975, four stamps honoring Contributors to the Cause were issued in four separate cities. Like the Postal Service Employees issue of 1973, each stamp bears a brief description of the subject on the reverse.

The bicentennial of the Battle of Lexington and Concord was marked April 19, 1975 by the release of a stamp based on the painting, "Birth of Liberty" by Henry Sandham, a painter of the period. Ceremonies held that day at Lexington and Concord included a reenactment of the events of 1775. First day of issue cancellations were available at each city.

A stamp based on John Trumbull's famous painting was released on June 17, 1975 to commemorate the Battle of Bunker Hill. Only the left portion of the painting was used. The right portion appeared in a 6c. stamp in the American Painting Series of 1968.

A block of four stamps depicting the uniforms worn by the Continental Army, Navy, Marines, and Militia during the Revolutionary War was issued on July 4, 1975.

On February 23, 1976 a sheet of 50 stamps was released, each stamp bearing the flag of an individual state of the U.S.

JULY 4,1776   JULY 4,1776   JULY 4,1776   JULY 4,1776

In the 1976 Declaration of Independence commemorative, four adjoining stamps make up the complete design of the famous John Trumbull painting.

A reproduction of John Trumbull's painting "Declaration of Independence" made its appearance on a strip of four 13c. stamps, appropriately enough, on July 4, 1976.

Other stamps in the American Bicentennial series include a May 4, 1978 13c. issue commemorating the bicentenary of the U.S.-French alliance, and the September 23, 1979 15c. specimen portraying Admiral John Paul Jones, along with the inscription, "I have not yet begun to fight."

The 1977 Skilled Hands of Independence issue acknowledge the civilian support represented by a seamstress, blacksmith, wheelwright and leatherworker to the winning of independence.

This souvenir sheet depicting Washington crossing the Delaware is one of four issued to coincide with the Seventh U.S. International Philatelic Exhibition.

These stamps reduced in size.

These innovative Bicentennial commemorative souvenir sheets contain five stamps each, perforated from the body of a patriotic painting reproduction.

The four sheets of five stamps each released to commemorate the INTERPHIL '76 exhibition are made up of large reproductions of famous patriotic paintings. Portions of the paintings have been perforated for use as stamps, each rectangular section including the denomination and the letters "USA".

The U.S. Postal Service has been more active than ever in issuing attractive multicolored stamps. Many are being produced in "se-tenant" blocks of four (se-tenant are groups of stamps in which there are at least two different designs in unseparated condition).

Many of the se-tenant blocks of four deal with specific aspects of Americana, including: "Pueblo Indian Pottery" (1977); "Skilled Hands for Independence" (1977); "American Quilts" (1978); "American Dance" (1978); "American Trees" (1978); "Pennsylvania Toleware" (1979); "American Architecture" (1979 and 1980); "American Indian Art" (1980); and "American Flowers" (1981).

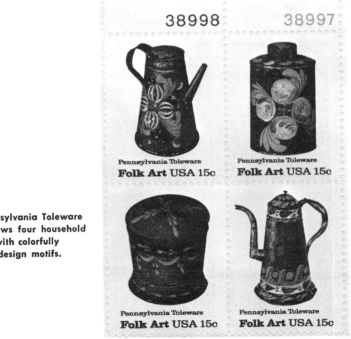

The Pennsylvania Toleware issue shows four household articles with colorfully painted design motifs.

39269 39268

Chilkat Tlingit
Indian Art USA 15c

Heiltsuk, Bella Bella
Indian Art USA 15c

Bella Coola
Indian Art USA 15c

Tlingit
Indian Art USA 15c

Many recent U.S. commemoratives have stamps of four or more different designs within the same sheet.

WHITE OAK
Quercus alba
USA 15c

GRAY BIRCH
Betula populifolia
USA 15c

38813

GIANT SEQUOIA
Sequoiadendron giganteum
USA 15c

WHITE PINE
Pinus strobus
USA 15c

© UNITED STATES POSTAL SERVICE 1978

These plate blocks of four in the American Architecture series were issued in 1979 (above) and 1980 (below). The buildings represent beauty, strength and usefulness.

Se-tenant blocks of four issued within the past five years depict other interesting facets of Americana, including: "Preservation of Wildlife Habitats" (1981); "American Architecture" (1981); "Desert Plants" (1981); "Knoxville World's Fair" (1982); "American Architecture" (1982); "Ballooning" (1983); "Los Angeles Summer Olympics," 13¢ values (1983); "American Inventors" (1983); "American Streetcars" (1983); "Sarajevo Winter Olympics," 20¢ values (1984); "Orchids" (1984); "Los Angeles Summer Olympics," 20¢ values (1984); "American Dogs" (1984); "American Folk Art," Duck Decoys (1985); "American Horses" (1985); "International Year of Youth" (1985); "American Folk Art," Woodcarved Figurines (1986); "Pathfinders of the North" (1986); "Lacemaking" (1987).

This partial sheet shows how the 1981 "Desert Plants" se-tenant set of four stamps is arranged.

The major theme at the Knoxville, Tennessee, 1982 World's Fair was energy and energy conservation, as illustrated in the above se-tenant block.

The "American Architecture" series now consists of four se-tenant blocks of four issued from 1979-1982. The latest in the series appears below.

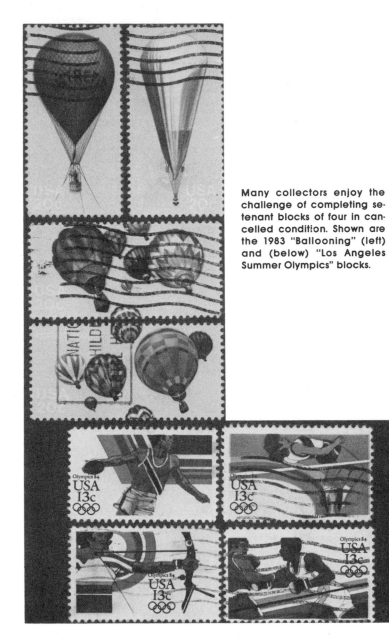

Many collectors enjoy the challenge of completing se-tenant blocks of four in can-celled condition. Shown are the 1983 "Ballooning" (left) and (below) "Los Angeles Summer Olympics" blocks.

Se-tenant blocks from the United States deal with an extraordinarily rich variety of topics. Shown above is the 1983 "American Inventors" series.

The "American Streetcars" block, also issued in 1983, is below.

Eight of the most popular canine types are featured in the 1984 "American Dogs" se-tenant block pictured above.

First-day ceremonies for the 1985 "American Horses" se-tenant block of four stamps were held at Lexington, Kentucky.

This unusual block of eight stamps was released in 1981 to mark U.S. achievements in space. They were issued in sheets containing six blocks.

Space achievements issue

A special se-tenant block of eight 18c. stamps issued by the U.S. Postal Service on May 21, 1981 at Kennedy Space Center in Florida honored American achievements in space. The format of the multicolored block is most unusual. Featured in the center of the design is a block of four stamps depicting the Space Shuttle "Columbia" taking off, being boosted into orbit, circling the earth, and landing. On either side of the block of four is a vertically oriented pair of smaller stamps highlighting other U.S. space achievements. At the upper right is the "Skylab" workshop and at the lower right is the Space Telescope, scheduled to be carried into space by the Space Shuttle in 1985. The stamps at the left side of the design feature the Apollo Moon Missions and Pioneer II. The vignette of the upper left stamp shows an astronaut walking on the moon. The lower left stamp shows the Pioneer II space vehicle. There are 48 stamps per pane with six complete se-tenant blocks of eight stamps per pane.

Single-stamp commemoratives

During the first half of the decade of the 1980s, the United States Postal Service produced commemoratives at an accelerated pace, turning out on the average some 50 varieties annually, a figure that does not include regulars, airmails, and special issues. Featured on the next three pages of illustrations are some of the most interesting of the single-stamp commemoratives, which treat as wide a variety of topics dealing with Americana as do the se-tenant blocks.

Shown in the first row, left to right: Helen Keller, renowned blind and deaf writer and lecturer taught by Anne Sullivan (1980); General Bernardo de Gálvez, who helped defeat the British in the Battle of Mobile, 1780 (1980); Everett Dirksen, U.S. Senator (1981); Edna St. Vincent Millay, poet (1981). Second row: Frederic Remington, sculptor, "Coming Through the Rye" (1981); James Hoban, Irish-American architect of the White House (1981).

First row (below): John Hanson, first president of the Continental Congress (1981); George Washington, 250th birthday anniversary (1982); "Performing Arts," actors John, Ethel and Lionel Barrymore (1982); American Libraries (1982). Second row: Touro Synagogue (1982); St. Francis of Assisi, 800th birthday anniversary (1982).

First row (below): Treaty of Amity and Commerce between USA and Sweden, 200th anniversary (1983); Civilian Conservation Corps, 50th anniversary (1983). Second row: Tennessee Valley Authority, 50th anniversary (1983); Physical Fitness (1983).

First row (top): Nathaniel Hawthorne, author (1983); "Love," issued for St. Valentine's Day (1984); "Performing Arts," Douglas Fairbanks, actor (1984); Jim Thorpe, athlete (1984). Second row: Herman Melville, author (1984); Horace Moses, founder of Junior Achievement (1984); "Performing Arts," Jerome Kern, composer (1985); "Black Heritage," Mary McLeod Bethune, author (1985). Third row: Rural Electrification Administration, 50th anniversary (1985); "AMERIPEX '86" (1985). Right: Arkansas Statehood Sesquicentennial (1986).

U.S. regular issues

Although millions of copies of each commemorative issue are printed, the supply is exhausted within a few months. However, the small convenient size regular issue stamps are available at post offices year in and year out in a range of values. The designs are changed occasionally, as when new rates go into effect, but they usually remain in use for years.

Following the Columbian Exposition commemoratives, the Bureau of Engraving and Printing took over stamp production from the private bank-note firms. Except for the "overrun countries" stamps of 1943-44, all U.S. stamps since 1894 have been printed at the Bureau. The first "Bureau issue" regular stamps were similar to the

The stamp at the left is part of the 1894 issue printed on unwatermarked paper. The one at the right, though the design is exactly the same, is from the 1895-98 issue printed on paper with a double line USPS watermark.

1890 bank-note issue. Triangle devices were added to the upper corners of the newer issue so they could be recognized easily but the portraits remained just about the same.

Counterfeit copies of the 2c. stamp were discovered in use during the next year, 1895. To make it easier to recognize counterfeits, the

The high values of the 1894 regular issue stamps carried portraits of Commodore Oliver Perry, hero of the 1813 Battle of Lake Erie, President James Madison and John Marshall, first Chief Justice of the United States.

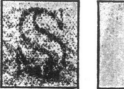

The two types of USPS watermarks used on U.S. postage stamps are double-lined capital letters with serifs and single line capital letters without serifs.

Bureau began printing the genuine stamps on a watermarked paper. The letters USPS were impressed in the paper during its manufacture. Where the design has been impressed, the paper is thinner and the watermark shows up when the paper is held in front of a

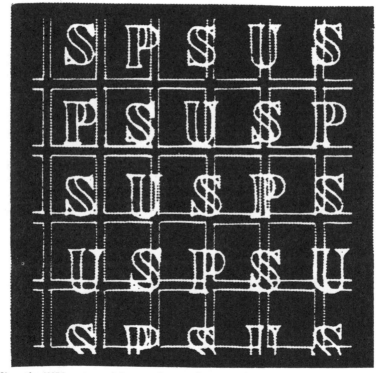

Since the USPS watermark is spread across the entire sheet, a full letter does not necessarily appear on any given stamp. Enough of a letter always shows, however, to determine whether a specimen is unwatermarked or carries a double or single line letter.

light. Watermarks are important to collectors because some designs, as in this case, are printed on both marked and unmarked paper, thus creating two different varieties. In other instances, the same design may appear on two or more differently watermarked papers. A difference in the quantities of each variety printed can cause an appreciable difference in value. With these designs, the unwatermarked varieties were produced for just one year, the watermarked stamps for 7 years. Now do you see why it costs more when you want to buy the unwatermarked varieties?

Most collectors content themselves with one example of each design, usually the least expensive variety. Advanced collectors who are specializing in United States stamps want a copy of every variety before they feel their collection is complete. Slight differences in design, shade and color are also the concern of the specialist.

Among the designs used on the issue of 1902-03 is the first appearance of Martha Washington on a stamp. Except for very elaborate new framework, the designs are about the same as the preceding issue. After so many years of picture gallery issues, the designers for the next issue switched back to Franklin and Washington who had been on the first stamps.

The stamps above illustrate perforation varieties of stamps with the same design. Varieties also occur because this same design was used on watermarked and unwatermarked paper and on two differently watermarked papers.

Outwardly the 1908-21 issue is a monotonous series with either Franklin or Washington on every one of the 19 denominations. Besides being printed on differently watermarked paper, much experimenting was done during these years with the gauge of the perforations. Otherwise identical stamps can be differentiated only by watermarks and/or perforations. The specialist collector recognizes no fewer than 178 varieties counting all of the watermark,

perforation, paper and printing differences. The "face different" collector satisfies himself with 27 stamps for the whole issue.

The long-lived designs of 1922-37 reverted once again to the earlier pattern, a series of distinguished Americans, including an Indian chief this time on the 14c. value. Some of the values show scenes of America; the Statue of Liberty, the Golden Gate, Niagara Falls, a bison, the Arlington Amphitheater, the Lincoln Memorial, the Capitol and the statue of America on the top of the dome.

Our most ambitious issue by far was the Presidential Series begun in 1938. All but three of its 32 values show portraits of former Presidents. The denominations through the 25c. stamps correspond to the order in which the Presidents held office; working this out created some strange denominations, the 16c., 18c., 19c., 21c.,

and 22c. values that had never been used before and really didn't serve much postal purpose.

The Patriotic series began appearing in 1954, gradually replacing the older Presidentials. Famous Americans and historic shrines were shown as well as former Presidents. The portraits were styled after contemporary paintings rather than formal busts. The structures shown include the Palace of the Governors built in Santa Fe in 1610, Mount Vernon, Bunker Hill monument, Andrew Jackson's home, the Hermitage, the Alamo, Independence Hall, and Thomas Jefferson's home, Monticello.

George Washington has appeared on more U.S. stamps than any other person.

124

The Patriotic series: 1954-1960

The next regular issue, the Prominent Americans series, made its debut in 1965. This series honors individuals who have made noteworthy contributions in a wide variety of fields, including government, science, industry and the arts. Among those portrayed are: Albert Gallatin, Treasury Secretary; Frank Lloyd Wright, architect; Francis Parkman, historian; Albert Einstein, scientist; Henry Ford, industrialist; Oliver Wendell Holmes, jurist; George C. Marshall, military leader and statesman; Frederick Douglass, editor and abolitionist; John Dewey, educator; Thomas Paine, author; Lucy Stone, social activist; Eugene O'Neill, playwright; and John Bassett Moore, jurist.

The 1970-74 Regular Issue series is a modest one consisting of only eight types. Dwight D. Eisenhower is portrayed on the 6c. and 8c. values, while the U.S. Postal Service emblem is shown on a second 8c. type. The 7c. denomination portrays Benjamin Franklin.

Others in the series are: Fiorello LaGuardia, Mayor of New York City; Ernie Pyle, Pulitzer Prize-winning World War II correspondent; Dr. Elizabeth Blackwell, first woman physician in the U.S.; and Amadeo P. Giannini, founder of the Bank of America.

The Americana series of 1975-81 was inspired by the Bicentennial celebrations, with the 20 values from 1c. to $5 depicting various

symbols of democracy, historic landmarks and other Americana. An early ballot box, the U.S. Eagle and Shield, and the head of the Statue of Liberty are among the symbols of democracy featured.

Among the many stamps featuring the American flag is this set of three with phrases from "America the Beautiful."

A set of three U.S. flag stamps was released on April 24, 1981 carrying phrases from the song "America the Beautiful." These were issued shortly after the first-class letter rate went to 18c. Because there have been so many increases in postal rates in recent years, the United States has had to issue a wide variety of new stamps reflecting those changes.

The 1980-85 "Great Americans" series consists of 25 denominations from 1¢ to 50¢, with a wide range of personalities being honored. Those portrayed in the first row (below) are: Dorothea Dix, social reformer and educator; Igor Stravinsky, composer; Henry Clay, statesman; Carl Schurz, journalist and statesman. Second row: Pearl Buck, Nobel Prize-winning author; Walter Lippmann, journalist; Abraham Baldwin, statesman and educator; Henry Knox, Revolutionary War general. Third row: Sylvanus Thayer, military engineer; Richard Russell, U.S. Senator; Alden Partridge, military educator; Chief Crazy Horse, Indian leader. Bottom row: Sinclair Lewis, Nobel Prize-winning novelist; Rachel Carson, author; George Mason, statesman; Sequoyah, Cherokee Indian educator and linguist.

First row (above): Ralph Bunche, Nobel Peace Prize-winner; Thomas H. Gallaudet, educator of the deaf; Harry S. Truman, 33rd U.S. President; John J. Audubon, ornithologist and illustrator. Second row: Frank C. Laubach, missionary and educator; Dr. Charles R. Drew, medical scientist; Robert Millikan, Nobel Prize-winning scientist; Grenville Clark, lawyer and author. Third row: Lillian M. Gilbreth, engineer and efficiency expert; and Admiral Chester W. Nimitz, World War II military leader.

The U.S. Postal Service's "Transportation" series of 1981–84, consisting of 14 denominations, all in coil form, was issued primarily for bulk-mailing purposes. Most of these varieties are available from post offices with precancels affixed by the Bureau of Engraving and Printing, Washington, D.C., and all portray some type of vintage conveyance. The "Transportation" series in coil form was expanded in 1985 with nine additional denominations. It is expected that additional vintage types of conveyances will be added in the future because postal rates are always changing.

The 1981-84 series features the following designs: First row: Omnibus, 1880s; Locomotive, 1870s; Handcar, 1880s. Second row: Stagecoach, 1890s; Motorcycle, 1913; Sleigh, 1880s. Third row: Bicycle, 1870s; Baby Buggy, 1880s; Mail Wagon, 1880s; Hansom Cab, 1890s. Fourth Row: Railroad Caboose, 1890s; Electric Auto, 1917; Surrey, 1890s; and Fire Pumper, 1860s.

The 1985 series features the following designs: First row: School Bus, 1920s; Buckboard, 1880s; Tricycle, 1880s. Second row: Ambulance, 1860s; Oil Wagon, 1890s; Stutz Bearcat, 1933. Third row: Stanley Steamer, 1909; Pushcart, 1880s; and Iceboat, 1880s.

In 1982 the "State Birds and Flowers" series became the U.S. Postal Service's second sheet of 50 stamps with 50 different designs. On this multicolored sheet of stamps—each with a 20¢ value—is a panorama of all of the 50 states' official birds and flowers, from Alabama to Wyoming. Some intrepid collectors try to get all 50 varieties in used condition with light cancellations.

Pictured below: Colorado (Lark Bunting & Rocky Mountain Columbine); Delaware (Blue Hen Chicken & Peach Blossom); Idaho (Mountain Bluebird & Syringa).

Illinois (Cardinal & Violet); Louisiana (Brown Pelican & Magnolia); Minnesota (Common Loon & Showy Lady Slipper).

Nebraska (Western Meadowlark & Goldenrod); New Mexico (Roadrunner & Yucca Flower); Oklahoma (Scissor-tailed Flycatcher & Mistletoe).

Pennsylvania (Ruffed Grouse & Mountain Laurel); Virginia (Cardinal & Flowering Dogwood); Wyoming (Western Meadowlark & Indian Paintbrush).

U.S. airpost issues

Whenever airmail stamps are mentioned, the world-famous "upside-down" airmail and the Graf Zeppelin issues come to mind. More stories and rumors have circulated about these two items than any other U.S. stamps, except perhaps the Columbians. Stamp dealers are frequently treated to stories about full sheets of these rare issues at home in the attic, but very few of them are ever produced.

The 24¢ value of the first airmail issue of 1918 shows a biplane printed in blue ink within a red frame.

The inverted airplane was found on just one sheet of 100 stamps of the 24c. value of the first airmail issue in 1918. Single copies of this stamp are worth over $100,000 today! The first airmail route was between New York and Washington, and now of course, every distant city can be reached by airmail.

One sheet of the 24¢ airmail stamps was issued with the airplane upside down. To print the two color stamps, the paper had to pass through the presses twice. The error was created when a sheet went through wrong end first for the second color.

This stamp enlarged.

Airmail stamps hold a special fascination for collectors; their exciting designs no doubt contribute to their popularity. One of the most exciting issues of all is the 1930 Graf Zeppelin issue of three values, 65c., $1.30 and $2.60. It is the prized possession of the few collectors fortunate enough to own the set. A set of mint copies of the three stamps sells for about $3,000, certainly a lot of money

The famous Graf Zeppelin issue of 1930 is the most sought-after of modern U.S. stamps. Large quantities of each denomination were printed but few collectors during the depression years were able to put away extra sets because of the high $4.55 face value. The unsold copies were destroyed after a few years and today the set of three stamps is worth nearly $3,000.00.

considering the face value of $4.55; yet, it has proved a good investment for those who have it. With new collectors constantly coming into the hobby, the price advances several dollars a year. Those who have had the pleasure of owning and displaying the set for a few years can now sell it for a profit.

The Wright brothers were honored on this 1949 6¢ airmail stamp commemorating the 50th anniversary of their famous flights. The plane is the "Kitty Hawk" whose first flight lasted only 12 seconds.

The DeHavilland biplane used on the first airmail stamp of 1918 was repeated on this 1968 issue honoring the 50th anniversary of airmail service. Modern presses print all the colors at once so this time no errors occurred.

This 26¢ international airmail stamp shows the Mt. Rushmore Memorial near Rapid City, South Dakota.

This stylized, white and blue design incorporates elements of the flag, an airplane and the two hemispheres.

The Pioneer Aviation series, begun in 1978 on the 75th anniversary of the Wright brothers' historic flight, honors the early flyers and designers. In the top row are Orville and Wilbur Wright and their Flyer biplane, Octave Chanute and his biplane hang-glider, and Wiley Post and the "Winnie Mae." In the bottom row are Blanche Stuart Scott, the first American woman to make a solo flight, and Glenn Curtiss, a noted designer and manufacturer.

In addition to the regular-issue se-tenant blocks, the U.S. released three sets of airmail se-tenant blocks of four in 1983 to publicize the 1984 Los Angeles Summer Olympics. These three airmail blocks appear in 28¢, 35¢, and 40¢ denominations.

In February 1985 the "Pioneer Aviation" series was resumed with the issuance of two additional stamps.

The 33¢ value (left) portrays Alfred V. Verville (1890-1970), aircraft designer.

Pictured in the 39¢ stamp is a dual portrait of Lawrence W. Sperry (1892-1931), designer and pilot, and his father, Elmer Sperry (1860-1930), inventor of aeronautical navigation equipment.

This 44¢ stamp (left) commemorates the 50th anniversary of transpacific aviation service.

The most recent U.S. airmail stamp (right) honors Junipero Serra (1713-84), the Spanish missionary who founded the first mission in the present state of California in San Diego.

Special delivery began in 1885 and distinctive stamps have been regularly issued for this service. The stamp combining special delivery and air mail rates was used only from 1934 through 1936.

Other classes of U.S. stamps include issues for special delivery, special delivery airmail, registered mail, certified mail, parcel post, special handling, postage due, official stamps, even overprints for

Distinctive parcel post stamps were issued in 1912-13 but, since then, regular issues have been used for this service.

post offices in China. Anyone specializing in United States stamps will surely want a U.S. specialty album to display them and a catalogue that tells the story behind each issue.

A series of regular issue stamps ranging from the 1¢ to $1 values were surcharged in 1919 for the U.S. postal agency in Shanghai, China. They were used for the pre-payment of postage on mail dispatched from China to addresses in the United States.

Collectors can add specialty items such as first-day covers, plate-number blocks and souvenir sheets to dress up their collections. Some collectors limit themselves only to these items.

Several special albums are available for the housing and display of U.S. stamps.

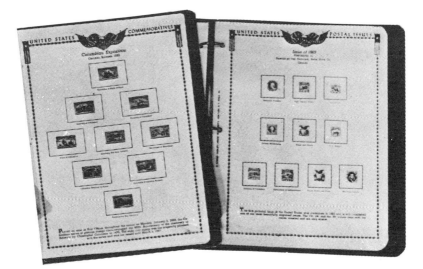

Album pages provide a space for each stamp plus a description and often a photograph of each issue. Many also present some historical background information.

The Bureau of Printing and Engraving puts a small number in the margin of each pane of stamps to indicate the plate from which it was printed. Collectors value the corner block of four with the margins and plate number intact.

These stamps reduced in size.

The United States Postal Service Information Service bulletins, available for a small fee from the Superintendent of Documents, Government Printing Office, Washington, D.C., 20402, include the details of the date of issue and the first-day city for each new stamp. To have covers serviced, you must forward self-addressed envelopes (standard size with a stiff filler) to the postmaster in the city designated for first-day sale. Payment for the stamps to be used must accompany your order in the form of a money order or

First Day Cover of the 4¢ Project Mercury commemorative. This is the only U.S. commemorative issued without advance notice. The stamps were prepared in secrecy and released in honor of the successful completion of the first American orbital flight.

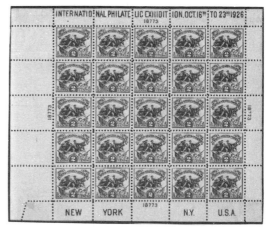

The U.S. Postal Service occasionally issues miniature souvenir sheets especially for stamp collectors.

a personal check. At least postage for the minimum first-class rate must be allowed for each envelope regardless of the denomination of the new stamp. The outside envelope containing your covers and order must be clearly marked FIRST-DAY COVERS. You should send your request about three weeks in advance and your order must be postmarked at least five days before the stamp is released. If you follow these instructions, your covers will arrive in the mail about two weeks after the stamp is released—the new stamp will be in the corner of each, neatly cancelled with the date, city and "First Day of Issue" imprint. Nearly every stamp dealer can supply you with serviced first-day covers, but it is fun to write for your own with blank first-day covers which are available from your dealer.

Your U.S. collection can be extended to include U.S. possessions, such as the Canal Zone, or the many foreign stamps which have been issued to honor Americans or commemorate events in American history.

7. United Kingdom Stamps

Great Britain stamps

Stamps of Great Britain traditionally have been designed in a very conservative fashion, but in recent years they have taken on greater panache and are often produced in many bright colors. Portraits of the monarch and the royal family no longer dominate the majority of stamp designs since the British Post Office now produces a wide variety of stamps dealing with all phases of English history and life. It is now customary to place the Queen's portrait in a small silhouette form in the stamp's upper right-hand corner.

The 1977 set (below), which depicts four racket sports (tennis, table tennis, squash, and badminton), commemorates the centenary of the Wimbledon Tennis Championships and the 1977 World Table Tennis Championships in Birmingham.

The 1980 set (above), portraying four different sports (track and field, rugby, boxing, and cricket) commemorates the centenaries of the Amateur Athletics Association, Welsh Rugby Union, and the Amateur Boxing Association, as well as the centenary of the first cricket match against Australia.

The "British Films" series, issued in 1985, is one of England's most attractive multicolored sets. Featured below are photographic portraits of the actors Peter Sellers and David Niven.

Also in the "British Films" series (above), the actress Vivien Leigh and the director Alfred Hitchcock. (The set also includes the actor Charles Chaplin.)

The 1985 "British Railways" series is a very collectible set of five (below): Flying Scotsman, Golden Arrow, Cheltenham Flyer, Royal Scot, and Cornish Riviera.

Canada

Canada released its first adhesive stamps in 1851, and, like Great Britain, for a very long time followed a highly conservative policy in producing new issues. However, in recent years Canada's postal designs have displayed greater flair and imagination. Moreover, commemoratives are being turned out with greater frequency. During the past decade, about 30 new commemoratives have been issued annually, most of them in multicolors.

Illustrated below are a few representative examples: (left) Royal Military College, Kingston, centennial (1976); (middle) The Iroquoians, from a set of four (1976); (right) Elizabeth II, Silver Jubilee (1977); (bottom) Ice Vessels (1978, setenant block).

(Top left) Niagara-on-the Lake, first capital of Upper Canada (1981); (Top right) New Brunswick, bicentennial (1984); (Right) Uranium Resources in Canada, 80th anniversary (1980).

Australia

Among the most interesting and colorful Australian stamp issues of recent years: (below) XII Commonwealth Games, Brisbane (1982).

(Left) Australian National Gallery, Canberra (1982); (middle) Australian Jaycees, 50th anniversary (1983); (right) Elizabeth II, 58th birthday (1984).

(Above) Los Angeles Summer Olympics (1984).

(Left, middle) Australia Day (1985); (right) Centenary of District Nursing Services (1985).

8. Topical Collections

Topical collecting is a branch of philately that is popular with many people who otherwise are not interested in stamps. Here is a kind of collecting without any "do's and don'ts." You choose a subject that appeals to your own interest, gather stamps from the nations of the world whose designs are related to your topic, and display them in whatever manner is most pleasing to you. In a topical collection, stamps are associated according to the subjects illustrated; the people, places or things pictured are somehow related to the subject you are collecting. Nearly every popular subject has been featured on stamps of many countries so your collection will have world-wide representation, yet be held within workable limits.

Sports, flowers and maps are popular subjects for topical collections.

Leafing through a stamp catalogue will suggest many different subjects; by studying the pictures, you can learn what stamps have been issued on any given topics. Watching the new issues of the world for designs appropriate to your collection will keep your enthusiasm at a high level. A topical collection, moreover, is always complete since each page or set of stamps is a unit by itself.

Choosing a subject to be developed is the first step. One may suggest itself from your work or some other personal interest—for example, athletes often select stamps with sports designs, doctors collect medicine on stamps, teachers and students can assemble stamps related to education. Every important human industry or

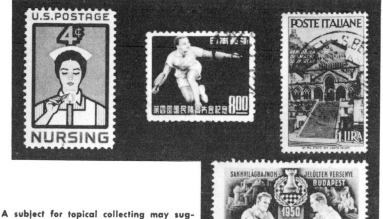

A subject for topical collecting may suggest itself from your personal interests; your work, sports, pastimes or travels.

resource is represented on postal issues. It's possible, on the other hand, that you may wish to break away from your everyday concerns and take up a topic such as flowers, birds, fish, animals, mountains or waterfalls because of the bright, beautiful, picturesque designs of these subjects.

Topical collecting in its simplest form is based entirely on the objects pictured on stamps. A design featuring an elephant or beaver or dog obviously belongs in an animals-on-stamps collection. Sometimes, though, your subject appears as just a small part of

This stamp fits into a collection of animals on stamps but it could also go into a collection of agriculture, plants or landscapes on stamps.

the over-all design, as the oxen on the British Guiana stamp shown on this page. You can decide for yourself whether you want such a stamp in a collection of animal stamps.

More elaborate topical collections are based on the themes expressed by stamps. Religion on stamps is a popular theme, and such a subject can be developed to include many kinds of stamps. Surely, stamps picturing churches and holy places belong in a religion-on-stamps collection, but you can add to these the hundreds of stamps picturing saints, religious leaders, composers of sacred music, reproductions of paintings of religious scenes and stamps such as the newly started U.S. Christmas issue—in other words, any stamps which refer to events of religious significance.

Events or anniversaries of world-wide importance are sometimes commemorated on stamps of several countries and make interesting topical collections in themselves. Recent occasions receiving world-wide recognition were the 100th anniversary of the Universal Postal

Sometimes many countries participate in stamp issues calling attention to occasions of world-wide significance.

Union, Rotary International's 50th anniversary, the International Geophysical Year, and the World Refugee Year. The United Nations and the Olympic Games are regularly topics of world-wide stamp releases.

Topical collections are displayed on blank album pages. Part of the fun of topical collecting is making pleasing arrangements of stamps on the pages. Most topics can be divided into groups and sections and the stamps of each group mounted together. If you collect animals, you might have one group for domestic animals, another for wild animals. Within each group, you might have a

separate page for each animal. A collector of trains on stamps would divide his collection into groups for steam engines, electric trains and diesel locomotives. Similar divisions suggest themselves for other topics.

Learn as much as you can about your topic and write a little caption below each stamp in your album. Your write-up should tell briefly the story behind the stamp as related to your particular topic. A world-wide stamp catalogue will give you information about the designs. To learn the historical background of your field, you will have to consult an encyclopedia and other such reference books. Stamps often fit into more than one kind of topical collection.

The choice of a topic for a specialized collection is practically unlimited. Topics such as outer space were not even thought of a few years ago. Now there are many stamps showing sputniks,

space capsules and communications satellites; undoubtedly, there are many more to come.

In recent years, specialized topicals have become extremely popular with collectors. We may call these specialty categories "subtopicals." For example, "Baseball on Stamps" is a sub-topical of

This large-sized Ras al Khaima airmail stamp commemorates the November 1969 Apollo XII mission to the moon by American astronauts. A suitable subject for a topical collection can be computers or space technology.

"Sports on Stamps." Other sub-topicals in this general area are "Basketball on Stamps," "Boxing on Stamps," "Cycling on Stamps," "Golf on Stamps," "Gymnastics on Stamps," "Hockey on Stamps," "Horse Racing on Stamps," "Soccer on Stamps," "Swimming and Water Sports on Stamps," "Tennis on Stamps," "Track and Field on Stamps," "Volleyball on Stamps," and "Wrestling on Stamps."

Since there have been so many thousands of sports stamps issued over the years, the energetic collector will have no difficulty in finding many stamps pertaining to each of these sub-topicals.

In regard to "Art on Stamps," the hobbyist may pick out one particular artistic style, or artists and their works from a single country: for example, Italian Renaissance art, French Impressionism, Spanish artists, or American artists. Or the collector may prefer to specialize in stamps dealing with a single major artist: *e.g.,* Leonardo da Vinci, El Greco, Goya, Michelangelo, Picasso, Raphael, Rembrandt, Rubens, Van Gogh, and others. For instance, if the hobbyist completes his assemblage of Picasso stamps, he can collect other artists like Michelangelo or Rembrandt. When he chooses a sub-topic he stands a better-than-even chance of attaining completion.

152

The American Topical Association (see page 188 for the A.T.A.'s address) has published hundreds of handbooks and monographs on every conceivable topic as an aid to collectors who strive for completion within given specialized areas.

Stamps illustrating the most popular topics are shown on the following pages.

Animals on Stamps

Art on Stamps

Baseball on Stamps

Birds on Stamps

Cats on Stamps

Children on Stamps

Costumes on Stamps

Dolls on Stamps

Fish on Stamps

Flowers on Stamps

Maps on Stamps

Medicine on Stamps

Music on Stamps

New York on Stamps

Petroleum Industry on Stamps

Picasso on Stamps

Religion on Stamps

Shells on Stamps

Ships on Stamps

Sports on Stamps

Stamps on Stamps

Trains on Stamps

Finding what stamps have been issued, getting the stamps you want, learning about them and mounting them in an album requires a great deal of time and study. Topical collecting can easily be your only collecting interest. On the other hand, it can provide an entertaining sideline to another specialty. You can keep busy with an elaborate topical collection or be equally pleased by the fun, attractiveness and interest of even a single simple topical project.

9. Buying and Selling

Acquiring stamps is one of the most important activities of collecting. Most of the wastebaskets around the country are already being watched for stamps, but you may still be fortunate enough to get stamps that way, or as outright gifts from friends and neighbors, or you can make occasional swaps with fellow collectors. The logical source for filling most of your empty spaces is the stamp dealer. Don't hesitate to buy stamps for your collection; all of us spend some money on the things we enjoy. If buying stamps gives you pleasure, it is every bit as reasonable as buying tickets to the movies or to a ball game—and you have something to show for it when it's over. By this time next year you will have forgotten who won the game, but stamps will still be in your album to enjoy. There is a good chance that you can later sell and recover some of the money you spent—perhaps even make a profit. Whoever heard of a refund for a used theatre ticket stub?

Stamp dealers

Dealers of all sorts are spread across the country and around the world. Larger cities all have stamp stores and literally thousands of mail-order dealers solicit business. Some carry a general line, others specialize, many ask for want lists, most will send approval assortments, and a few sell only at auction. Something can be said for the largest and smallest dealers. Big dealers have world-wide resources for getting the stamps you want, but the smaller dealer can get to know you more intimately. He has the time to give you personal attention.

If you have a local stamp store, it's a good idea to try there first. Most dealers started out as collectors and have spent a lot of time studying stamps and their background. Because you are a potential customer, they will be glad to give you help with your collection. Being collectors at heart, too, most dealers like to talk about their hobby, stamps, and will be glad to help you even if you are not likely to become their biggest customer. Seeing stamps on display at a retail shop will teach you a considerable amount about the kinds of stamps available, what the issues of different countries look like, and what they cost. You can also learn a lot by reading stamp ads.

Buying by mail

Mail-order dealers advertise in newspapers, national magazines, even on match-book covers. The stamp magazines and newspapers listed in the next chapter are full of dealers' ads. Stamp ads frequently offer premiums known as loss-leaders to attract new customers. Ads offering attractive assortments for just a few cents generally specify "with approvals" or "approvals accompany" which means that in addition to the item you order the dealer is going to send you a selection of other stamps at regular prices that he hopes you will buy. This is not a bad thing since it gives you a chance to see many more stamps, especially when it is not handy for you to visit a stamp store. You are not under obligation to buy from these approvals, but the dealer hopes you will. It's a great temptation to send 10c. for every bargain you see offered, but resist it unless you are willing to look over the other merchandise and possibly give the dealer some additional business. If you have too many approvals coming in at one time, it's difficult to decide what to keep and you probably will not buy enough from any one lot to justify the dealer's expense in making up and sending the selection.

Approvals

Looking through approval selections is a good way to fill in empty spaces, once you have assembled the bulk of your collection from packets. There is no difficulty in finding dealers who will send you stamps "on approval." Don't request them from too many companies at the same time, though; you get much better service and assortments when you are known as a regular customer. If you are more interested in stamps of certain countries or if you want only new or used stamps (used are generally less expensive), be sure to tell the approval dealer—he will prepare his selections to suit your wants. The big advantage of approval buying is that you have

177

the privilege of examining many stamps before you pay for any. The disadvantage is that it is costly for dealers to prepare and process approvals, and this is reflected in the prices you have to pay.

Approval stamps are usually mounted on sheets with the catalogue number and price of each stamp clearly marked. Sometimes the prices are for sets of stamps which are not to be broken. Remove the stamps you want to buy and return the rest along with payment for the ones you keep. Beginners' lots usually contain stamps priced from 2c. to 10c. each. You are expected to make your return and remittance within 10 days. You must pay for any stamps that are lost or damaged while in your possession, and it goes without saying that you are not to trade or substitute stamps.

Some dealers offer "penny approvals." Stamps at this price are haphazardly mounted on sheets or loose in envelopes. They are not identified by catalogue number and there are none of the data you sometimes get with more expensive approvals. Doing some of the dealer's work yourself, however, brings the price down low. Stamps in these selections are usually not in as good condition as regular approvals and many dealers are now charging 2c. or more for their "penny approvals"—but still inexpensive enough.

Unsolicited approvals

As a result of answering ads or sending for a price list, your name may get on a mailing list and you will receive approval selections without having ordered them from companies you've never heard of. Sending "unsolicited approvals" is a practice many collectors condemn, but you may be interested in the stamps and appreciate the service. Keep in mind that you are not under obligation to buy from an approval selection if you don't want to, especially if you haven't asked for it. If the dealer who sends you unsolicited approvals doesn't include return postage, you legally don't have to return them. However if you receive approvals that you don't request and aren't interested in buying, the best idea is to return them, whether postage is provided or not, with a note telling the dealer you are returning the stamps this time, but not to send any more. If more are sent after this, just put the lot aside and ignore it until the dealer sends you postage for its return. If you don't buy, you will soon enough be off the prospect list. As you might imagine, dealers in this business have a high rate of loss and must charge sufficiently high prices for the stamps they do sell to make up for the ones that are never paid for.

Buying from ads and price lists

Ordering specific stamps from ads or printed price lists is about the best way to fill spaces at low cost. As we have seen, preparation of approval selections is time-consuming for the dealer and he must make up for his time in the prices he asks. Paid-in-advance orders for special stamps can be handled at much lower cost and the saving is passed on to the customer. The dealer has invested money in his ad or price list and will make his prices low enough to ensure getting enough business as a result. Not only that but prices listed in print are easily compared with what other dealers charge for the same stamps, so the dealer will be sure the prices he quotes are as low as anyone's. To order from ads, you must subscribe or have access to stamp papers or magazines, and you need a catalogue to know what is being offered. Lengthy descriptions are costly so the dealer usually gives just the catalogue number, the condition and the price asked. Unless they specify otherwise, the numbers used in ads are taken from the Scott Standard Postage Stamp Catalogue. You are expected to send payment with your order and to keep the stamps unless they are not as advertised. Any unsatisfactory stamps should be returned without delay.

Stamp stores

Check your classified telephone directory under "Postage Stamp Dealers" for the addresses of local stores. At stamp stores you can buy stamps in mixtures, packets and sets, as well as single stamps. You will also see many specialty items such as covers, maximum cards and souvenir sheets. No doubt you are already well acquainted with packets and will be more interested in the stock books. This is the place to look once you have assembled the bulk of your collection and are trying to fill in spaces. Stock books are usually arranged by country and the dealer puts in all of the miscellaneous stamps he gets from the collections he buys and breaks up. You will find both mint and used stamps in these books and frequently

179

more than one copy of the same stamp. If the dealer lets you pick the one you want, remember what you have learned about condition and look for the best one. Don't be too long in looking them over, though, or the dealer will feel he's wasting time waiting for you to choose and will just hand you one stamp. If the dealer is doing the selecting, don't hesitate to ask if he has another copy, if you don't like the first stamp he offers.

Mint sets

Mint sets of related stamps issued at the same time are sold as a complete unit with every value from the highest to the lowest. If the set 'contains expensive high values, dealers usually offer a modestly priced alternative, a "short set" complete except for the top values. Before you buy a complete set, check to see whether your album has spaces for all values or just the short set. Complete sets of mint stamps, especially commemoratives, have the best investment potential.

Want lists

If the stamps you want don't turn up in approval selections and you cannot find them in dealers' ads and price lists or their stock books, you can try leaving your dealer a want list. Give him a list of stamps that you're looking for—catalogue number and condition wanted, whether new or used, premium copy or average stamp—and he will try to get them for you from other dealers, and will also watch for them among the stamps passing through his hands. As they are available, he will submit stamps against your list. You can return any that do not suit you because of condition or other factors, but you are under a little more obligation to buy when you ask for specific items as opposed to general approvals. The dealer has devoted more time to finding your particular stamps and you should repay him with a purchase whenever possible. Topical collectors often must use want lists to get the stamps they want.

New issues

Many collectors find it convenient to place standing orders for all new issues from their favorite countries and their dealer sends stamps automatically as he gets them in stock. Dealers' first stock of new issues frequently sell out; by placing a standing order, you are assured of getting every issue you want at the lowest first price.

Specialized dealers

Collectors who specialize may not be able to get all the stamps they want from general dealers. No one dealer can possibly have every variety of every stamp of every country. Topical collectors especially run into trouble since many of the stamps showing the subjects they're interested in are in the middle of sets and regular dealers are reluctant to break them. Dealers specializing in topicals stock individual stamps.

If you collect stamps from just one country and want varieties or older issues, you may have to get them from a specialist. Other specialist dealers feature covers, precancels, plate blocks; whatever your collecting interest, there is a dealer to serve you.

Buying at auction

Stamp auctions are conducted frequently but feature only medium- or high-priced stamps. If there are common stamps included, they are lumped together in lots. Sales are well advertised in advance and you can write for a catalogue if you are interested. At public auctions you can enter bids from the floor. Mail bidders fill out a bid sheet showing their maximum offer per lot. To bid intelligently you must be familiar with stamps and their values and be able to estimate how lots will sell. All sales are final, unless you can show a lot was improperly catalogued (which seldom happens), so auctions are a little risky for beginners.

Stamp agencies

Unless you are buying in quantity for investment, service charges make it more expensive to buy stamps direct from foreign countries than from your local dealer. The United States, United Nations and Canadian Philatelic Agencies are easy to deal with and all will supply current unused stamps of good quality. For information on available stamps write:

Philatelic Agency, U.S. Postal Service, Washington, D.C. 20265

Philatelic Section, Financial Division, Post Office Department, Ottawa, Canada KIA OB5

United Nations Postal Administration, United Nations, New York, NY 10022

Stamps of some Latin American countries are available from the Organization of American States, Washington, D.C. 20006. If you want to try ordering direct from abroad, address an inquiry to the Director of Posts, Post Office Department, c/o the capital city of the country. You are most likely to get replies from European countries, most of whom are accustomed to dealing with collectors. Payment should be made by international money order that you can purchase at your local post office.

Club circuit books

Some clubs provide this service—members mount duplicates in books provided by the club, a price is put on each stamp by its owner and the books circulate among the other club members who remove any stamps they wish to buy. The book plus remittance is then returned to the club member in charge of books. A small percentage goes to the club to defray the expense of handling. This works well for the seller because he gets money for his duplicates but is even better for the buyer since the prices are well below what he would pay at retail.

Trading

Stamps are generally traded on the basis of catalogue value rather than one for one. Joining a stamp club (as urged in the next chapter) is one of many ways to contact people who will trade duplicates with you. It's also possible to correspond with collectors here and in foreign countries who will trade stamps. Stamp papers have subscribers all over the world and inserting a small classified ad will surely get some response—or you can watch for ads that other collectors run. You can also write to the U.S. government's People-to-People Letter Exchange Program, Box 1201, Kansas City, Missouri, 66117, or the People-to-People Hobbies Committee, 85 Canisteo Street, Hornell, NY 14843, for the names of people in other countries who want to exchange stamps.

Foreign embassies here or our embassies abroad may give you the names of people in other countries who will trade stamps—or at least they may reward your inquiry by using foreign stamps on their reply envelope.

Investment

Stamp values are determined by supply and demand. If a new issue is in short supply and demand for the stamps is strong, its price invariably goes up. On the contrary, if too many of a stamp are printed or if too many people buy up the same issue, the likelihood of making a profit within a reasonable time is poor.

When you first start collecting, you should buy a stamp mainly because it appeals to you and fits in with your collection, not because you think it is a way to make money. Nevertheless, you don't want to buy blindly and you should exercise the same care with stamp purchases that you use with any other. Here are some worthwhile thoughts to keep in mind when buying stamps.

Don't be carried away by a wave of popularity for certain issues. Some recent issues hit a peak price while they were in the spotlight and interest was heavy. As collectors moved on to the next new issue, interest lagged and prices dropped. Too often, highly promoted issues are popular today, forgotten tomorrow. Be cautious, especially about issues with paid publicity behind them. The smart buyer bides his time, passing the highly touted issues in preference to bargains that are being overlooked in the excitement of getting on the bandwagon.

Sets of mint stamps have the best investment potential. Commemoratives or other limited issues are better than regular issues which may be produced for years. Commemoratives are generally released just once in predetermined limited quantity, the plates then destroyed, and no more is ever printed. The original printing minus the number used for postage is the total number of stamps available to satisfy the demands of collectors forever. Each day new collectors take up the hobby, and this creates a growing demand for a steadily diminishing supply of stamps, a sure omen of price increases ahead.

Stamps from popular countries are likely to remain in demand over the years. It's not wise to invest unless there is a steady demand for a country's issues because there won't be anyone to buy them when you are ready to sell. If the designs show animals, flowers, sports or other popular subjects, you will have a two-fold demand for them—from collectors of that country's issues, as well as from topical specialists. Color and design have nothing to do with a stamp's historical significance, but it is a fact that bright, attractive stamps are in greater demand than plain ones. If you are buying for investment, the event a stamp commemorates becomes secondary to its attractiveness, the number issued and the demand for it.

Prices

How do you know whether a dealer's prices are fair? This is not as much a problem as you might think. There is so much competition in the stamp trade that dealers seldom last long if their prices are too far out of line. If you want to check up on someone, though, study the advertised prices of a popular item (use one that several dealers quote prices on in the same week) and compare them with what your dealer wants for the same thing. Don't expect him to undersell every one every time, but if he is consistently above average, then you should look around.

Catalogues provide a par value for each stamp. The market price may be over or under the catalogue value, according to its current popularity. A great many stamps can be purchased below catalogue. If they're far below, it's because there is little demand for them and they are likely to stay about the same price over the years— which means they are poor investments if you want to make a profit. It also means that you can take your time about buying such stamps if you want them for your collection.

Prices of some stamps seem to advance out of all proportion to their catalogue values. The only explanation for this is that they are in vogue at the moment. The majority of stamps, however, advance normally in keeping with the increasing number of collectors.

Selling stamps

Offering stamps for sale is often a disillusioning experience for collectors. It shouldn't be, if you remember certain facts. Every time you buy a stamp the price you pay includes a mark-up for the dealer to provide him with a reasonable profit on the transaction after covering the cost of his services, and his overhead in maintaining a business. Unless the value of your stamps has gone up, you can't resell them for the price you paid. A dealer buying from you must allow for the same expenses of overhead, and of carrying the purchased stamps in stock until a buyer is found. Also, he has the cost of advertising, plus the need for a profit for the time he will spend incorporating your collections into his stock.

Outright sale

Selling a collection outright to a dealer is the fastest way to get your money. Be sure your stamps look their best before you offer them. Pull out any torn, mutilated, heavily cancelled or otherwise undesirable stamps. You won't get a cent for them and they will make your good stamps look worse. Give the impression of being a collector who bought only good stamps and the dealer will have more respect for you and your collection. Be sure every stamp is in its proper place as the buyer will be much more interested if he notes that he can put your material right into stock without further checking.

Don't hesitate to quote a figure if you are asked how much you want. No doubt the prospective buyer will say it is too much, but the counter-offer he makes will very likely be better than if you leave it to him to state a first figure. Don't ask for a ridiculous amount, however, or you will give the impression that you don't know anything about stamp values.

In an outright cash sale to a dealer, you should not expect more than about 50% of the selling price of complete mint sets and as little as 20%-25% of your cost if you have a general collection made up of packet material. Much of what you paid for packets went towards the cost of making them up.

It is foolish to sell for a small fraction of your cost, especially if your only reason for selling is that your interest in collecting has lagged—in a few years you may wish you had your stamps back.

Consignment sale

Stamps sold on consignments are catalogued and priced by their owner and turned over to a dealer who in turn offers them to his regular customers. At the end of a specified period, the dealer returns any remaining stamps and pays for the ones sold. He deducts his commission at a rate which has been agreed upon in advance. Dealers ask a commission ranging from 15% to 25% of the selling price depending upon how valuable and readily saleable your stamps are.

The advantage of consignment selling is that you can get the price you want for your stamps if they are sold at all. The disadvantage is that you have to wait for the final settlement to get your money. For another thing, you may find only your best stamps were sold and what is left over isn't worth anything without the better items to attract some interest.

Sale at auction

This is the most important means for disposing of valuable stamps. The competition among bidders sets the price, so that only those stamps in considerable demand sell well at auction. Common stamps that are normally offered by any dealer sell at very low prices when put up at auction since nothing about them excites the bidders' enthusiasm.

For selling valuable stamps, auction is best since the catalogue circulates to a wider audience than one dealer can possibly reach. The owner gets more in the long run since the commission for cataloguing and selling is only 15-25% and good stamps sell at the highest possible price. However, there may be a delay of as much as six months from the time the material is submitted, until the auction is held and payment received from buyers. You also must agree to sell to the highest bidder and you must accept the risk of a disappointing sale price. In recent years, commission rates charged to the seller have gone down because some auction houses are now charging the buyer a 10% fee on the knockdown price.

10. Stamp Clubs, Newspapers and Magazines

Joining a stamp club is the way to ensure a lively, continuing interest in your collection. Just being able to talk stamps with like-minded people will renew your enthusiasm. You will meet experienced collectors, some of whom are probably working on projects similar to your own and can give you valuable advice and suggestions.

Exhibits and displays are an important feature of club meetings; as a fellow hobbyist, you can appreciate the effort others put into their collections and you will discover the pleasure of displaying and telling about your own possessions. Besides the educational merit of belonging to a club, there is the valuable opportunity of trading duplicates—getting rid of excess stamps in exchange for stamps you want. Many full-time stamp dealers got their start buying and selling at club meetings.

Stamp collectors are nearly always nice, friendly people who are worth meeting for their own sake aside from any benefits you might receive. Across the country are thousands of stamp clubs and all of them welcome new members. You can find out about their meetings by watching your local paper for announcements of meetings, writing to the stamp editor if your paper has a column, inquiring at the community center, YMCA, or by asking your stamp dealer or postmaster. The advantages of membership are worth the effort of joining.

National associations

In addition to local groups there are several national societies organized for the advancement of philately. A beginning collector gets more benefit from a local group, but the national societies are worthwhile for collectors at all levels. You should consider joining one of the national societies right away if no local club is available.

For membership information write:

The American Philatelic Society,
P.O. Box 800,
State College, Pa. 16801

American Airmail Society,
P.O. Box 40463
Indianapolis, Ind. 46240

The Philatelic Foundation
270 Madison Ave.
New York, N.Y. 10016

American Topical Association,
P.O. Box 630
Johnstown, Pa. 15907

Newspapers and magazines

Subscribing to one of the frequently published stamp papers is the only way to keep up with events in the stamp world. In them, you will find timely material and new discoveries, first-day releases, announcements of world-wide new issues, as well as interesting articles on all phases of collecting. Every issue carries dealers' buy-and-sell advertising, so that you can make contacts to fill your needs or to sell your stamps. Any of the following will send you a sample copy on request:

Stamp Collector (weekly), $17.00 per year
Albany, Ore. 97321

Linn's Weekly Stamp news (weekly), $22.95 per year
P.O. Box 29,
Sidney, Ohio 45367

Stamps (weekly), $16.50 per year
85 Canisteo Street
Hornell, NY 14843

Scott's Monthly Stamp Journal, $18.00 per year
P.O. Box 29
Sidney, Ohio 45367

Index

loss-leaders, 177

maps on stamps, 164
"margin" of a stamp, 16, 140
mark-up, dealer, 185
maximum cards, 79, 179
medicine on stamps, 165
"mint" condition, 17, 179, 180, 183
mixtures
    "off paper," 25, 179
    "on paper," 25, 179
moon, post office on the, 99
mounting stamps, 12, 14
music on stamps, 166

newspaper stamps, 20
New York on stamps, 167

occupation stamps, 22, 23
"official" stamps, 22
"on approval" stamps, 13
order, systematic, 6
overprints, 22, 23, 38, 138

packets, 24, 179
parcel post, 20, 138
Penny Black, 7
"penny stamps," 13, 178
perforations, 16, 17
periodicals, stamp, 188
petroleum industry on stamps, 168
philatelic groups, 6
philately, 15
Picasso on stamps, 169
plate-number blocks, 81, 138, 181
pneumatic stamps, 20
poor, 78
    see also condition of stamps
postmarks, 34
precancelled stamps, 23, 181
price lists from dealers, 179
"provisionals," 20

rare varieties, 13
registered mail, 20, 138
religion on stamps, 170
resale, 5
"roulette" stamps, 16, 17

sales, stamp, 181
"secret marks," 86
self-adhesive stamp, first, 101

semi-postal stamps, 21
"se-tenant" blocks, 107-114
shapes of stamps, 15
shells on stamps, 171
ships on stamps, 172
"short set," 180
sizes of stamps, 15, 16
soaking, 34
societies, national stamp, 187, 188
souvenir sheets, 138, 141, 179
special delivery stamps, 19, 138
special handling stamps, 20
specialization in collecting, 24, 70
    albums for, list of, 72
    by dealers, 176
    popular countries, 70, 71
sports on stamps, 173
stamps on stamps, 174
stock books, dealer's, 179
superb, 76, 77
    see also condition of stamps
surcharge, 22
swapping stamps, 12

tongs, 13, 31, 66.
topical collections, 148-175
trains on stamps, 175
twin stamps, 96

United Kingdom stamps, 142-144
United States stamps, 82-141
unused stamps, working with, 31, 69
upgrading of collection, 68
used stamps, 17, 179
U.S. Postal Service Information
    Service, 140

value, monetary, of stamps, 13
very fine, 77
    see also condition of stamps

want lists, 180
watermarks, 18, 32, 121, 122
    USPS, 120
watermark tray, 75
working with stamps
    alphabetizing, 35
    identifying, 35, 38
    selecting a workplace, 34
    sorting, 34
    verifying, 37